Katrine Martensen-Larsen

NORDIC COLOURS

HOW TO CREATE INTERIOR MOODS

LANNOO

PREFACE

Katrine Martensen-Larsen

When I began my journey as an interior stylist over twenty years ago, I lacked skill in sketching by hand and navigating complex software. Relying on my rudimentary hand-drawn sketches, I could envision harmonious forms and colours, yet convincing others of my design choices proved challenging. Faced with complex renovations, I desperately needed a tool to provide cohesion throughout the project and keep track of the myriad decisions to be made.

If drawing is not an option, how can we test whether colours, patterns, materials, and textures complement each other, clash, or simply do not work together? How do we convey ideas and concepts to clients, partners, contractors, design advisers, or those selling us furniture, paint, wallpaper, and curtains?

The answer lies in mood boards, a simple and accessible tool for everyone. Mood boards are collages of colours, fabrics, wallpapers, wood, leather, stone, tiles, metals, and carpets—a mosaic of material samples that evoke a distinct feeling, ambience, and style. While you can create mood boards digitally using platforms like Houzz or Pinterest, I find physical mood boards to be far more effective. I cherish the tactile quality, the sensory experience, and particularly the creative process of juxtaposing different samples on a fabric-covered board. There's a unique magic that happens when everything suddenly falls into place.

In my previous book, *Nordic Moods – A Guide to Successful Interior Decoration*, published first in Denmark in 2018 and then globally by Lannoo, I introduced this practical tool. I guided readers in discovering their personal decorating style and provided step-by-step instructions on creating their own mood boards. I explained their applications, the materials needed, and how to work with them.

I also invited readers into nine Nordic homes, each reflecting the owner's ability to craft a beautiful and personalised environment. I firmly believe that a home is most intriguing when its design clearly reflects its inhabitants. It is less about what is considered beautiful or ugly, or which style is currently in vogue, and more about creating moods and achieving harmony.

Between each home feature, I addressed common design challenges. Themes such as the art of limitation, furniture placement and proportions, lighting, curtains, carpets, and the personal touches that come from art and crafts were explored.

In this book, I focus on how to integrate colour into your home. Colour has an incredible power to shape mood. In the Nordic region, monochromatic palettes—greys, whites, blacks, beige, and brown tones—have dominated for many years. While this palette is easy to work with and hard to get wrong, there's always a counter-reaction. Recently, colour has made a vibrant comeback in interior design, encouraging bold experimentation, though results can vary.

Through my experience as an interior designer, I've learned that many people find choosing colours one of the most daunting tasks. How do you find the right comfortable, tasteful, lively, and harmonious palette? How can you avoid making your home resemble a playschool classroom? And how do you ensure aesthetics remain inviting rather than overwhelming? As you may have guessed, the solution lies in mood boards.

I will begin by briefly revisiting how to work with mood boards, then guide you to discover your own colour palette and highlight important aspects to consider when living with colour. Just like in *Nordic Moods*, you will be welcomed into nine personal homes where the common thread in this edition is colour. Each home's style is summarised on a mood board, and between each feature, I will delve into methods for infusing colour into your interior. Topics such as painting and wallpaper, soft furnishings, curtains, art, collectibles, books, rugs, plants and flowers, wood, and stone will be addressed.

In the world of interior design, colour is not merely a choice, but an expression of our identities, emotions, and aspirations. In this book, I aim to explore this vital element and enhance our living spaces through the artful use of colour. Colours are not a fixed or static choice; they shift depending on the materials to which they are applied, and the same colour can appear very different depending on the material or surface it is used on, whether it is plaster, clay, wood, stone, textile, or leather.

Colours also change significantly depending on the light in a given room. Whether a living room is bathed in sunlight or sits in the shade facing north will decisively influence the perception of a given colour. The rhythm of the day and the changing of the seasons also leave a clear mark on the colours we surround ourselves with.

Colours shift from hue to hue - reflected in the tones of walls and wood, the nuances of an artwork they stand against, and in ceramics, glass, pillows, rugs, and throws. And last but not least, colours change over time. They acquire patina, wear, fade, and bleach.

I celebrate all of it - the idea that a colour is not just a colour, but a complex and changing dimension. With this exploration of colour, I invite you to transform your living spaces into vibrant reflections of who you are, embracing the beauty of diversity and the art of harmonious design.

CONTENTS

THE CREATIVE PROCESS

Before introducing you to the nine Nordic, specifically Danish homes, each of which has successfully tackled the challenging task of colour in its own unique way, I will briefly review how to work with mood boards. I will also guide you in discovering your own colour palette and the important factors to consider when wanting to surround yourself with colour.

WORKING WITH MOOD BOARDS

Working with mood boards is an effective method, whether you want to enhance an existing design or start from scratch. You can create your mood boards on a fabric-covered board, which is convenient if you want the flexibility to rearrange them. In *Nordic Moods*, I provided a step-by-step guide on how to create mood boards yourself. If you haven't got a bulletin board available, you can also lay your material samples directly on the floor or a rug, but remember to choose a surface that is representative of the space(s) you wish to design.

ENHANCING AN EXISTING DESIGN

Imagine you need to reupholster a sofa in your current home or purchase a new armchair. Should you choose leather or fabric? Solid colour, striped, or patterned? You are faced with an important decision and a significant investment, so you can't afford to make the wrong choice.

What you can do is gather samples from your existing decor—your floor, wall colour, curtains, the material of your coffee table, and textiles or leather from other furniture in the room. Place as many materials from the space as possible on your board, and test them against the various fabric and leather samples you are considering for reupholstering your sofa or for the new armchair. You can use the same approach if you want to change the wall colour or replace curtains. You'll be surprised at how much easier the choice becomes.

Remember that prominent pieces of art can have a very dominating effect in your space, so always ensure that the colours in your home's artwork harmonise with the other colour elements in the decor. It is impossible to select wall colours without keeping the artwork in mind.

STARTING FROM SCRATCH

Imagine now that you are about to renovate an entirely new home or perhaps even build a new house from the ground up. What materials should you choose, and where do you begin? What kind of flooring will you select? What type of kitchen do you dream of? What style, materials, countertops, fixtures, tiles, and door handles? Once you have made all the foundational choices and are ready to tackle the fun aspects—wall colours, curtains, furniture, and lighting—what should you choose? Many people feel so exhausted at this stage that the final important selections become quick, disappointing choices.

There are a lot of tasteful and appealing designs on the market, and it can be tempting to get carried away. However, there is also plenty of the opposite. It is crucial to realise that you cannot—and should not—merge a multitude of styles within a single home. Choosing one direction and style means simultaneously rejecting another. Otherwise, you end up with a chaotic mix of everything, lacking clear direction. I call this 'the art of limitation'.

My recommendation is to start with the large surfaces, such as the flooring. I often say that you should invest as much as possible in your floors. It's similar to your wardrobe: you might be wearing the most expensive dress, but shabby shoes will ruin the entire look. Floors are also difficult to change once you've moved in, so making the right choice here is absolutely essential.

What type of flooring do you prefer: wood, terrazzo, tiles, linoleum, or concrete? What feels pleasant to walk on, provides good acoustics, and is practical? These are all factors you need to consider. I also recommend having consistently uniform flooring throughout the entire home, as this creates a calm and harmonious foundation. You may get away with using just two different types, such as wood in the living areas and tiles in the entryway and bathroom. The kitchen floor can be either wood or tiles, depending on your taste, but it should match the wood from the living areas or the tiles from the bathroom. Be sure to obtain a material sample of your chosen flooring and place it as the first element on your mood board. You can then move on to doors and panelling and later to walls and ceilings.

It can be beautiful to paint doors and panelling in a different colour if the walls are white, or vice versa. Wooden doors and panelling can also be extremely lovely. Before making final decisions, remember to place material samples on your mood board.

If your walls are made of drywall, they can be wallpapered or painted. But walls can also be made of concrete or wood, both of which will add colour, character, and texture to the decor. Most homes feature white-painted ceilings of drywall or plaster. However, ceiling surfaces can also be painted in other colours or consist of different materials, as you will see later in the book. Again, place the colour and material samples on your mood board and evaluate them.

You may now be at the stage of selecting materials for your furnishings, such as the fronts of kitchen cabinets and other storage units. If you have chosen wooden flooring, painted fronts can create an elegant look. If you have opted for stone floors, it might be fitting to use organic material, such as wood, for the fronts. But what colour? What type of wood? And what type of finish: oil, lacquer, or soap? Experiment with these options on your mood board.

Consider what you personally like. Think about the practicality of the different types of finishes and also consider what types of wood your other furniture pieces are made from. For instance, if your dining table or chairs are made of oak, it could be beautiful to continue this wood type through your shelves, cabinets, and fronts.

To achieve a cohesive look, I recommend incorporating a variety of materials and surfaces into your design. Wood, stone, painted surfaces, metal, textiles, leather, and fur should all be represented. However, it is less important which materials are used where. If your sofa has a fabric covering, you can choose leather for an armchair. If your coffee table is made of stone, your dining table can be wood. Having all seating in the same colour leather, on the other hand, can be visually less interesting, much like using the same shape for all tables in your home. It is all about variation and the right mix.

NORDIC COLOURS

Nordic colours refer to a specific palette we often use in Scandinavia. Our design is characterised by simplicity, functionality, and a strong connection to nature. The colour scheme often includes soft, muted tones inspired by the natural landscapes in our latitudes.

Common Nordic colours include:

- ***Whites and off-whites:*** these create a clean and airy feel, often used as a base
- ***Greys:*** soft greys represent the stone and rocky areas of the landscape
- ***Blues:*** various shades of blue evoke the sea and sky, ranging from light pastels to deeper navy tones
- ***Earthy tones:*** browns, taupes, and muted greens reflect the forested and natural environments
- ***Accent colours:*** while the base is often neutral, brighter accents in colours like mustard yellows, deep reds, or soft pinks may be added to bring warmth and personality

COLOUR THEORY

Finding the right colour palette for your home begins with a foundational understanding of colour theory, which can guide you in your choices and help create the desired atmosphere. Colours are not just visual elements; they have deep emotional and psychological effects that can influence our mood and well-being.

In this context, the Bauhaus movement, founded in the early 20th century, played a crucial role in modern design and colour theory. One of its prominent figures, Johannes Itten, emphasised the importance of colour in art and design. He developed the concept of the colour wheel and identified the 12 colours along with seven contrast categories, which have become fundamental in understanding how colours interact.

Colours can be divided into three main categories: primary, secondary, and tertiary colours. The primary colours—red, yellow, and blue—cannot be created by mixing other colours. When primary colours are combined, they form secondary colours: green (blue + yellow), orange (red + yellow), and purple (blue + red). Tertiary colours are achieved by mixing a primary with a secondary colour, resulting in shades like red-orange and blue-green.

Itten's ideas also introduced us to warm and cool colour classifications. Warm colours, such as red, orange, and yellow, promote a sense of energy, vitality, and closeness, evoking feelings of joy and enthusiasm. Cool colours, including blue, green, and purple, have a calming effect, promoting peace, tranquillity, and introspection. Balancing warm and cool colours in your home can create a dynamic and harmonious atmosphere.

Contrasts are another essential aspect of colour theory. Complementary colours, which are directly opposite each other on the colour wheel, create visual tension and interest. For example, the powerful red colour beautifully contrasts with its complementary green hue. Including such contrasts in your decor can highlight specific details and create visual drama. Meanwhile, analogous colours, which are adjacent on the colour wheel, such as blue, blue-green, and green, can create a gentle and cohesive palette, resulting in a seamless feeling and an inviting space.

The quest for the perfect colour palette is not merely an aesthetic journey but also an emotional one. It is important to consider how colours interact with the light in the room since lighting can alter how colours are perceived. Natural light often enhances the warmth and nuance of colours, while artificial light can provide a completely different experience. By understanding these basic principles, you can begin to explore which colours resonate with you and how they can be combined to form a cohesive colour palette for your interior design.

HOW TO FIND THE RIGHT COLOUR SCHEME

Finding the right colour palette is a personal journey. You need to find the colours that not only look good together but also evoke the feelings and moods you wish to achieve in your home. It's essential that you thrive, gain energy, find peace, and achieve whatever you desire from your interior design. When it comes to colour choices, just like everything else in your home, the primary consideration should be your own preferences. Remember that.

If you find it difficult to choose colours, rest assured, you are not alone. The process can be both challenging and time-consuming, and it's important to expect a fair amount of experimentation before everything clicks into place. A well-curated colour palette is crucial for creating a harmonious and, in my view, successful interior. If the colour scheme is discordant or cluttered, even the loveliest furniture and artworks in the most stylish spaces will not work effectively. I would wager that you wouldn't feel comfortable either. Therefore, it is vital to invest the necessary time and effort in finding the right colours for your home.

When I talk about using a colour palette, I mean that merely selecting a single colour for each room or for your home is far from sufficient. Generally, you should use three to five colours per room. It's the collective colours across all rooms that together form your unique palette.

If you prefer a neutral colour theme, you can blend several shades, such as off-white, beige, brown, grey, mocha, sand, mustard, and black, more freely than if you wish to work with bolder colours. In that case, I suggest you limit yourself to a maximum of three colours—perhaps a blueish, a greenish, and a greyish tone, or a reddish, a yellowish, and a brownish one. If you're feeling adventurous, you might even allow one of the three colours to stand out more prominently or add a contrast colour.

The colours in your interior typically consist of wall colours, ceiling colours, trim colours, and the fabrics of your sofa or armchair. However, colours can also come from dining tables, chairs, and other small pieces of furniture, as well as from rugs, cushions, throws, curtains, and lamps. Additionally, there will be colours from wooden furniture, wood floors, and tiles, as well as from artwork, crafts, books, and plants, among other sources. In later chapters, I will delve deeper into many of these topics, but for now, let's focus on which colours should be included.

It may be a good idea to study Itten's colour wheel and the seven contrasts, so acquire a colour fan (with large swatches) and start considering which colours you personally like and look at the contrasting colours. Maybe this can provide you with some inspiration.

The pure colours in Itten's colour wheel are referred to as saturated, but they can also be mixed with white or black, in which case they are called broken or unsaturated. I would recommend choosing more muted tones than those you find in Itten's colour wheel, but the principle of having a contrasting colour remains the same. If you get a colour fan from a paint manufacturer, they will automatically be much more subdued.

Now simply select some colours from your fan and see if they complement each other. Think about the atmosphere you want in your home and how colours can significantly affect your mood. For example, I personally cannot live with strong red colours, as they feel heavy and claustrophobic to me. In contrast, I feel uplifted and in a good mood with blue and greenish aqua colours.

Practically speaking, you can take the colours you like, along with any potential contrasting colours, from your fan and lay them out on a mood board or simply on the floor in your living room, bedroom, kitchen, or whichever room you are about to decorate. If multiple rooms or your entire home need to be styled, I recommend creating a board for each room and laying them side by side. A good idea is to try to create a common thread throughout the spaces. You may like all colours, but as with styles, you cannot incorporate everything into a single design.

You should choose a primary colour for each room by considering what constitutes the largest surfaces in the various rooms. In the living room, it is typically the floors, walls, and ceilings, and possibly the sofa, which is often the largest piece of furniture. In the bedroom, it may again be the walls, but the surface of the bed can be significant as well. In the bathroom, the wall surfaces in the shower niche may stand out; perhaps this is where the primary colour for the room should be placed.

In addition, you will need to select a couple of secondary colours and a contrast colour. Secondary colours can include the colours of woodwork, cushions, throws, and curtains. I personally almost always use black as a contrast colour; it can appear on lamps, chairs, or tabletops. A contrast colour can also come from materials such as chrome, brushed steel, or brass in fixtures, handles, or lamps.

A good tip is to let a secondary colour in one room become the primary colour in the next. This way, you carry a colour with you from one room to another, which will create a harmonious and cohesive experience.

In general, I stay away from bright signal colours and prefer low-saturated, muted, and slightly greyed or dirty colours. Colours that are difficult to define and change with the light make them more interesting and pleasant: a grey-green, a pink-brown, a mustard-yellow—notice how I need to use several words to describe the colours I want to have in my home. These are often colours that have been mixed with black. If you enjoy cool blues, greys, and greens, look for variations within that scale. Take them out of the colour fan and place them on your mood boards.

If you are fortunate enough to own some artwork that you cherish, you should take the time to study it closely before choosing your colour palette. Often, this is where you can unlock the code for the colours that will work best together in your space. I have frequently based my colour choices on a piece of art and encouraged my clients to do the same. I typically point out areas in a painting where multiple tones flow in and out of each other, emphasising that this is precisely where you can find the colours to focus on. As long as you select wall colours, textiles, and decor that harmonise with the colours present in this area or throughout the entire painting, it will always work. It doesn't necessarily have to be the most striking colour in the artwork; it can just as well be some of the background colours.

When choosing colours, I also find great inspiration by looking out the windows. What colours do you see on the buildings across the street? What colours are present in your garden or on your property? This approach can often be effective and ensure that your colour palette is harmonious and integrates well with the surroundings.

If you're at a complete loss, take a trip into nature. Pick a beautiful flower, such as a hydrangea, and let it dry. You will be surprised by the beautiful colours that emerge as it fades. The combination of a primary colour in the flower's head and a secondary colour on the stem can be ideal—and crafted by nature.

THE 60-30-10 RULE

The 60–30–10 rule is a classic guideline in interior design that helps create a harmonious balance of colours within a space. By using colours in a proportion of 60%, 30%, and 10%, you establish a visual hierarchy that guides the eye and enhances the overall aesthetic of your environment.

60% dominant hue: The foundation of your colour palette is the dominant hue, which should occupy approximately 60% of the space. This colour is typically used for walls, larger furniture pieces, and flooring, providing a cohesive backdrop that sets the tone for the entire room. Choosing a neutral or calming colour for this percentage allows for versatility and depth, creating a comfortable and inviting atmosphere.

30% secondary colour: The secondary colour makes up about 30% of the palette and is crucial for adding depth and interest. This colour is often applied to upholstery, drapery, or accent furniture. The secondary colour should complement the dominant hue, enhancing the overall colour scheme while introducing variation. This balance helps to avoid monotony and encourages the eye to take in the space more fully.

10% accent colour: The final 10% is designated to accent colours, which should be used sparingly to add pops of interest and excitement to the room. Accent colours can appear in decorative accessories such as scatter cushions, artwork, vases, or rugs. These vibrant touches are essential for creating focal points and can evoke a sense of personality and style. While the accent colour is typically bolder or more saturated than the other colours, it should harmonise with both the dominant and secondary colours to enhance the overall palette.

The success of the 60–30–10 rule lies in its ability to guide the eye comfortably from one element to the next, promoting a fluid movement throughout the space. This balance creates visual rhythm and harmony, making the environment feel well thought-out and cohesive. Even if your palette contains more than three colours (but ideally no more than five), adhering to this proportional guideline will help maintain balance. By thoughtfully distributing your colours using the 60–30–10 rule, you can transform a room into a harmonious and inviting space that reflects your personal style.

9 NORDIC HOMES AND 9 WAYS TO ADD COLOUR

Colour in interior design can originate from various sources beyond just painted walls and wallpaper. While curtains, upholstery, cushions, throws, and especially artwork offer excellent opportunities for adding colour, hues in a home can also arise from building materials like wood, stone, and tiles, as well as from collectibles, books, flowers, and plants. Let's take a tour of nine distinct Danish homes, where the owners have thoughtfully curated their colour palettes and achieved impressive results through diverse methods. In intermezzos, I will explore the specific techniques they have employed.

COLOUR EXTRAVAGANZA

"Over the years, I have become increasingly passionate about colours, and I wanted to use them in a new and different way," explains Sara Lysgaard, who lives with her extensive art collection in a modern two-storey villa just north of Copenhagen. The art collection has been beautifully complemented by vibrant colours on the walls, ceilings, woodwork, and furniture, as well as cushions and throws. Sara is not too proud to admit that she sought advice from a professional because she wanted to create something truly extraordinary. That professional was none other than my brother, Jannik Martensen-Larsen, whose bold approach to colour in decor surpasses my own.

MOOD BOARD

An abundance of art and a spectrum of colours await as soon as you step into Sara's home. Bold greens, turquoises, reds, blues, and yellows playfully compete with her impressive collection of contemporary art.

The entire ceiling of the ground floor is painted in a light arsenic hue that gracefully extends down a portion of the wall, meeting a deeper green tone. The many terrace doors are finished in a dusty crimson red, while the kitchen window frames and the wall piece opposite the fireplace are painted in a striking saffron yellow. A soft blue guides you to the first floor, where the bedrooms are adorned in deep navy blue and lush green, respectively.

The furnishings in the expansive open dining and living area comprise a delightful mix of Danish and Italian classics, including a large round Poul Kjærholm table with a marble top and an ash ring, surrounded by delicately painted Y chairs in a soft grey-green, accented with woven seats. The iconic Italian Camaleonda sofa boasts beautiful upholstery of mustard velour complemented by cognac leather, while the daybed is dressed in a vibrant yellow. Adding to this are cushions upholstered in a charming mix of patterns featuring small checks, botanical motifs, and a zigzag print, along with a pink wool throw. The small round coffee tables by English designer McCollin Bryan, featuring brass frames with resin tops in sapphire and emerald colours, shine brightly in the sunlight that pours into the corner of the living room, making them reminiscent of exquisite vintage glass marbles.

On the floor, wide oak planks and Moroccan Beni Ouarain rugs with geometric patterns coexist harmoniously. The jewel of the living room is the stunning large artwork, *Milky Way* by Troels Carlsen, in an impressive wenge frame. Also commanding attention is a tall ceramic lamp base adorned with turquoise harlequin patterns, and an array of vintage footballs cascading down from a net hanging from the ceiling, while a wild dandelion bursts through the floor behind the dining table.

On paper, it may sound wild and eccentric, but Sara and Jannik demonstrate that there are no strict rules when it comes to decorating with art and colour. If you are skilled, courageous, and confident, then anything is possible.

STRIKING COLOURS TO COMPLEMENT IMPRESSIVE ART

The art in the home ranges widely, from Dario Escobar's net of vintage footballs gracefully draping down the staircase to large figurative works by Carlos Armorales and Troels Carlsen, while photographic art by Ugo Rondinone elegantly wraps around a corner in the living room. Tactile pieces by Julie Lænkholm, Justin Morin, and Adam Jeppesen adorn the bedroom and dressing room, alongside ceramic works by Cathrine Raben Davidsen, Morten Løpner Esbensen, and Camilla Skov. Neon installations by Gun Gordillo, as well as objects by Tony Matelli, Karl Monies, and Claudia Comte, also feature prominently.

Sara began curating her art collection as a teenager, with her first encounter with art being a piece by Poul Gadegaard. Geometric in form and painted in shades of red, blue, green, and gold, she vividly remembers it from her childhood home, where modern art was as natural a part of the interior as a bed or sofa.

"The artists have something they want to tell us, and what they do is not just for fun," Sara explains. "I feel extremely privileged to surround myself with all these aesthetic works and thoughtfully crafted things. Take the footballs, for instance. They represent the underside of real footballs, and what Dario Escobar wants to convey is that in the world of sports, everyone is equal; it doesn't matter if you are born rich or poor—you have the opportunity to make something of yourself."

The works in Sara's collection are like a visual diary of her life. She can return to each piece and recall the situation and mood she was in when she acquired it. "When the artworks come home, my life with them begins. It's not so much that I have a dialogue with them; it's more of an embrace and the emotional atmosphere they create when I wake up in the morning and see them. I can truly feel them—a lot."

ARCANA

Sara purchased her first piece with her childhood savings at Galerie Moderne, accompanied by her father. It was a work by the English artist David Spiller. Today, she travels the world exploring art. I ask her, as a serious art collector, how it works: "I keep an eye out. I attend fairs, visit artists, and receive invitations to numerous previews. Staying informed is crucial. It gets serious the moment you run out of wall space but continue to buy. When you have to find art storage somewhere, that's when it becomes serious in a different way."

I ask what she looks for when purchasing a new piece of art. "As my collection has grown, I've begun to see some patterns emerging—a common thread. For me to buy a new piece, I need to feel that it fits in. Another observation I've made is that the more I see, the less I tend to like. I can appreciate something's beauty, but it simply doesn't belong in my collection, and I never make impulsive purchases."

When Sara buys art, it's because a piece resonates with her emotionally—something that transcends all logic. In those moments, she doesn't consider where it will hang, where the artist has exhibited, or which collections they belong to. She also puts aside thoughts about the price (within reason, of course). When rational considerations are set aside, "It often happens quickly. Either it's there, or it's not, but I've also experienced that an artist can grow on me. For example, it took a while for me to connect with Troels Carlsen's work. The same went for Julie Lænkholm's. Suddenly, it just clicked."

Sara perceptively recognises that her impressive art collection should be complemented by equally striking colours. "It has been revitalising for me to live with colours that interact with my works. I feel my pieces gain 'new life' when placed on a coloured wall. It's akin to giving your plants fresh soil; something new can flourish when a piece is combined with a wall colour. There are endless possibilities to breathe 'new life' into a work by painting your walls in fresh colours. I love the idea of infinity in this; it's like it never really ends, and there are always new combinations to explore. An extended present."

SHARE

THOUGHTS

THO
UG

Sara Lysgaard

Beyond her passion for art, Sara dedicates much of her time to investing in startups and companies focused on green transformation. A few years ago, she also invested in the art magazine *Ark Journal*, which has achieved remarkable international success in a very short time.

"I've realised that I don't need to do everything myself. Instead, I've chosen to take a backseat and let others pick up the baton. I can contribute my time, strategic input, and financial support, and in the case of *Ark Journal*, I've also found a platform to channel good stories from the art world."

Together with Luise Gomard, and Tania and Thomas Asbæk, Sara has recently opened Kunsthal n, a new art hall in Nørrebro, Copenhagen, located in an old printing house within one of the district's historical buildings. Kunsthal n showcases international art with a focus on contemporary art that actively reflects, shapes, and drives the narrative of humanity today. The art hall operates as a non-profit organisation, aiming to establish educational programmes for schoolchildren while opening up and democratising the art world by offering free admission.

“If I were to describe a general theme of my art and my use of colours, it would be the pursuing of the potential of life. Paint in a tube is by default fascinating to look at. But nothing interesting ever comes to life if it remains in its factory settings. Paint, in that way, is similar to human existence. You can make something valuable out of it, if you try hard.”

–

Troels Carlsen (1973), Danish Painter

INTERMEZZO

Paint

In the introductory section, 'How to Find the Right Colour Scheme', I recommended using three to five colours for each room you plan to decorate. Choose a **primary colour** that constitutes about 60% of the space, a couple of **secondary colours** that together make up approximately 30%, and one or two **accent colours** for the remaining 10%. If you're decorating multiple rooms in a home, it's wise to let some of these colours reappear from room to room. This way, you won't have to reinvent the wheel in every space, and the colour repetition will create a natural and calming visual flow throughout the home.

Typically, the **wall colour** becomes the primary colour in a room, simply because walls cover the largest surface area. For instance, you might vary the primary colour from room to room while keeping the secondary colours consistent. You could use the same colour for woodwork throughout the home and the same colour for the ceilings.

If you decide to change the colours of the woodwork and ceilings from room to room, you're embarking on an advanced project that requires careful consideration. The more you switch colours between rooms, the higher the risk of creating a chaotic and disharmonious look, but it also increases the potential for something bold and unconventional. If you're confident in your choices, go for it! However, if you prefer tranquillity and harmony, use the same colour for **woodwork and ceilings** throughout the home.

Wall colours are generally easier to experiment with, and if you're not set on having uniform wall colours in every room (such as white walls), I strongly advocate painting your walls in different colours. Personally, I prefer muted non-colours in a completely **matte finish**. A coloured wall also better highlights the fine details of white-painted woodwork and ceiling mouldings.

A sophisticated alternative is to paint the woodwork in the same colour as the walls, a trend that has become quite popular in recent years and can look very elegant. You could opt for completely matte paint for both walls and woodwork, or you may choose to increase the sheen on the woodwork to vary the expression. Here, you'll need to **experiment to find what works** best for you.

Painting ceilings in colour can also be tasteful and impactful, and I've seen some very successful examples of this. However, it does require a bit more courage and a discerning eye for colour. (See Colour Extravaganza, p.36 and Island Delight, p.60-78)

When selecting paint for your home, it's crucial to examine the colours while in the rooms you intend to paint. **Light and surroundings** can change dramatically, and the colour you like in one place may appear entirely different in another. To ensure great results, purchase a small sample pot of the colours you're considering and test them on all north, south, east, and west-facing walls in the room—and possibly on the ceiling. Paint an area about 50x50 cm, applying two to three coats, and then assess the colours in both natural and artificial lighting.

If in doubt, get some additional samples. Try a lighter and darker shade of the colour you're considering and paint similar wall samples. Remember to **note the colour codes** during this process. Consider the colours at different times of the day as well. This process can be time-consuming, but it's essential.

Don't forget to coordinate your colour choices with your **art and furniture**. If you have a specific artwork or upholstered furniture that you know will be part of the space, begin by matching the colour to these central elements—ideally on your mood board. Additionally, if your rooms have other defining factors (like wood, a stone floor, or a carpet), you should closely examine how your chosen colours relate to those elements.

2

ISLAND DELIGHT

This charming little townhouse in Ærøskøbing is an example of an interior design project based on thorough groundwork with mood boards. The house, originally built in 1827, was purchased around five years ago by my cousin Louise Harder and her husband Thomas Fischer, who were fully aware that everything would need renovation. Fortunately, the couple had teamed up with an exceptionally skilled architect, so the floor plan was well organised. I was tasked with selecting colours, choosing materials for surfaces and furnishings, and assisting with the subsequent interior decoration.

When the couple took over the house, the outside was yellow with faded green doors and window frames, but whether it would remain that way was far from certain. We were at a complete loss, and the brief was as follows: "We want something extraordinary. There should be many colours, and we won't compromise on anything. We need a practical floor in the kitchen and a huge gas stove, because we love to cook."

MOOD BOARD

The little townhouse now features newly constructed half-timbering and red-flecked brick panels, with petroleum-green woodwork and white accents around the casement windows. Inside, we have indulged in soft and delicate Nordic tones—Inchyra Blue, Pavilion Grey, Dead Salmon, Oval Room Blue, Preference Red, Treron, and Pigeon adorn the walls and ceilings, with several being executed in traditional techniques referred to as Ærø listelofter, as well as on all custom-built furnishings. The solid panel doors, frames, and mouldings, recreated based on the original designs, have been painted in Hardwick White. For some, this may conjure thoughts of liquorice confection, which is not all that far off.

The exposed beam construction inside has been stripped of old paint, revealing striking contrasts that testify to the building's age and craftsmanship. The floors feature narrow, white-oiled pine planks in the living rooms and bedrooms, while the hall, kitchen, pantry, bathrooms, and the entire courtyard are paved with delicate yellow tiles in a bond pattern.

A single guest room and the house's home office are wallpapered in two different colour versions—seafoam and moss green—of the same striped design, Ribbon, complemented by matching textiles for the curtains, cushions, and headboard. Behind the voluminous gas stove in the kitchen are tiles featuring a simple, decorative, and deliberately disruptive pattern of green and black on a delicate cream background.

As the finishing touch, ink on silk art by Helene Blanche features dreamy motifs with nods to Japanese art where light and shadow meet in inner imagery. Sometimes dark and intensely deep colours; at other times light and spherical, before being succeeded by soft repetitive patterns in multiple dimensions.

A HOUSE WITHOUT A SINGLE WHITE SURFACE

A share in Ærø Whisky, costing 1,000 kroner, a birthday gift from Louise to Thomas in 2014, was life-changing for the couple. Louise had seen a feature on TV2, where the late Danish Prince Henrik and Queen Margrethe II visited the newly established whisky distillery in the courtyard of a merchant's house.

The gift was well received. So much so that Thomas and Louise soon took a weekend trip to the South Funen Archipelago and, along with a couple of friends and business associates, shortly thereafter decided to invest a bit more money in the whisky project. But Louise and Thomas also fell in love with a small townhouse with holiday home status.

Holidays and many weekends were now spent on the island of Ærø, and gradually the couple became so involved in the cultural life there that the little house in the town of Ærøskøbing had to be replaced with a larger home with year-round status. They chose the house next to the town museum on Nørregade, with the caveat that the house would need a total renovation. The couple hired FAVN architecture from Svendborg and building constructor Simon Katborg Davidsen from 360 BygRåd, and once the drawings and municipal approval were in place, I was invited to Ærø to discuss colours and material choices.

After visiting the house, which honestly looked somewhat worn, we took a walk around the picturesque town for inspiration. Ærøskøbing is a charming town located on the island of Ærø, known for its well-preserved historic centre with narrow streets, pastel-coloured houses, and cobbled roads that create a picturesque atmosphere. The town has a rich maritime cultural history and has been an important port city for centuries.

I was particularly taken with the faded green front door of the newly purchased old townhouse, and when I photographed it, the colour appeared more petroleum-like in the picture than in reality. That colour stuck in my mind, and when I later spotted it on another property in the town, covered in a lovely dark red, ideas began to take shape.

We continued our stroll through the town, and I suggested we visit the town's most prominent building—the beautiful Ærøskøbing Church. I was on a mission to find some authentic colour combinations to use as inspiration. In the church, I was delighted to see that the old benches were painted in the exact same faded petroleum colour. This colour was now set; I would use it on the exterior doors and window frames as well as all other external woodwork, and I would carry it inside to the new wood panels in the entrance and the staircase's balusters. It was a slightly daring and dark colour, but exclusive and beautiful. The first difficult piece of the puzzle was now in place.

What I also noticed in Ærøskøbing Church was the beautiful floor made of yellow tiles. Louise and Thomas were looking for practical flooring and had already discussed tiles. We all agreed to proceed with this idea, and my suggestion was to lay tiles in the entrance, kitchen, and utility room, as well as in the laundry room, on the floors of both bathrooms, and out into the courtyard. In the bedrooms and living room, we would have an authentic wooden floor made of informal pine planks—not too wide, as the house is narrow, and we didn't want to lay down anything other than what could have been an original solution. This way, we managed to stick to two different types of flooring in and around the house.

During our tour of the town, we also stopped by Ærø Whisky Distillery and Hattesens Lakridskonfektfabrik, both local businesses in which Louise and Thomas had invested. We only received samples at the latter, the liquorice factory, but both places provided me with plenty of eye candy. I was particularly inspired by the upcoming colour design task at the confectionery factory.

We returned to the house, where demolition was in full swing, and looked at some colours from my Farrow & Ball colour palette. It was difficult to see how they would fit in the house because all the windows were covered with plastic, and the only lighting was coming from powerful work lamps. We stepped outside to capture the daylight and quickly settled on a greyish beige woodwork colour, agreeing that there should not be a single white surface in the house when we were finished. Louise and Thomas wanted original Ærø listelofter—painted in delightful colours. I made a note of that.

Back home in Copenhagen, I set about creating a colour plan for the entire house. Specifically, I made a series of boards: one large one to encompass all materials and elements in the house's biggest room—the kitchen-living area, and several smaller ones—one for each bedroom, one for the living room, one for the office, and one for each bathroom. I laid these mood boards on the floor of my creative workshop so I could see and work on them in context.

I decided to use the same overarching woodwork colour throughout the house (the tertiary colour) and to paint both walls and ceilings in different colours in all rooms. Each room was assigned a primary colour for the walls and a secondary colour for the ceiling. Furthermore, all rooms that would be furnished with built-in furniture received an additional secondary colour. Beyond the petroleum-green, I would introduce contrasting colours through lamps, handles, and fixtures, as well as later through art and crafts.

The interior beam construction on the level separation, as well as specific walls and the actual roof construction, were exposed, and I recommended removing the old paint from the beams. This turned out to be a costly and time-consuming affair, as the painters had to wrap the wood in brown soap up to five times. But the result is outstanding.

As an interesting detail, I chose to have the ceiling colour in the kitchen-living area become the wall colour in an adjacent bedroom. The wall colour in this bedroom then continued into the next room as the striped colour in a wallpaper and in the matching textile I chose for the curtains, bedspreads, pillows, and shower curtains. And so forth. This was because I wanted to carry a colour from each room into the next to create a common thread. There's something new each time you step into a room, but you shouldn't suddenly have to deal with a completely new palette.

Oh, what a joy it has been to work with such a competent architect and builder, such sublime craftspeople, and - last but not least - clients who made their choices and never changed their mind along the way. A client with courage for colours and the resources to not compromise at all.

JAZZ
ANDELEN
RØSKØBING

Louise Harder and Thomas Fischer

Thomas Fischer is a prominent figure in Danish business, known for his role as co-founder of the consulting firm Valcon, which specialises in optimising business performance. Throughout his career, he has built extensive experience in strategy, business development, and leadership.

Today, he is also an investor and owner of several companies. Together with Louise, he has invested in Ærø Whisky, where he contributes to developing the distillery's innovative approach to whisky production and focus on quality. Moreover, the couple is involved in Hattesens Lakridskonfektfabrik, known for their high-quality handmade liquorice products.

In addition to his investments in these companies, Thomas also serves as the chairman of Hotel Sanders, a luxury hotel chain in Denmark, and is a newly appointed member of the board at Kvadrat Acoustics, a recognised Danish producer of textiles and design products.

Louise is a researcher, section leader, and lecturer at the IT University of Copenhagen. She has a PhD in technology implementation and focuses on how technology can be used to improve user experiences and create innovative solutions. In addition to her professional work, Louise is the vice chair of the Ærø Jazz Festival Association, one of Denmark's oldest jazz festivals that each summer creates a vibrant atmosphere with performances from both Danish and international jazz musicians throughout Ærøskøbing.

"What I love about using colour is the ability to elevate a room or simply create emotional and physical responses within that space. How a splash of yellow, maybe a ceramic lamp or a lacquered coffee table, can bring joy to a more soberly decorated room or finding the perfect green for a bedroom to help one relax and sleep. I also love the potential that colour, especially paint and papers, can totally transform a room without the need to change anything else, maybe reposition some furniture and re-hang your artwork, but two coats of a new colour or an elegant wallpaper can give a new lease of life to a room."

–

Patrick O'Donnell (1968), International Brand Ambassador at Farrow & Ball

INTERMEZZO

Wallpaper

If you want to add some flair to your walls, consider using wallpaper **in a few select rooms**. However, if you wallpaper every room in your home with different patterns, it can quickly turn into a chaotic mix, reminiscent of a charming yet aesthetically lacking English countryside bed and breakfast.

Ideally, the wallpaper you choose should incorporate some of the other colours in the room, as well as colours from adjoining spaces. If your walls feel bare, wallpaper can effectively make your home feel **warm and inviting**.

In my opinion, wallpaper works best in areas like entryways, bedrooms, children's rooms, or guest bathrooms. The latter is particularly clever; since you only spend a short time in the room, you won't become bored with the wallpaper. You can truly turn up the **wow factor** here, opting for a bold design that surprises your guests (see Colour Extravaganza, p.33).

I never recommend wallpapering living rooms in private homes. I prefer **artwork on the walls instead**, as having both can create a cluttered look. In hotels, cafes, restaurants, or other public spaces, the situation is different because there may not be other suitable items to hang. In such cases, wallpaper is an effective and low-cost way to set the mood.

Be aware that wallpaper can easily become overwhelming, and removing it can be a hassle if you tire of it. Remember, the surface of the wall you wish to wallpaper should be just as smooth as if you were painting it. **Wallpapering is no shortcut** to avoid the tedious work of preparing walls; imperfections will show through.

When selecting wallpaper, pay special attention to how it fits into your **overall colour scheme**. It can be beautiful to see through doorways to a wallpapered area where one of the wall colours reappears. Also, note that the background colour in a **patterned wallpaper** is often not pure white and may appear dirty against freshly painted white woodwork and ceilings. Instead, consider painting the ceilings and woodwork in the wallpaper's off-white base colour or one of the other colours from the pattern. It's a good idea to choose wallpaper and wall, ceiling, and woodwork colours together in a cohesive moment. If you find this overwhelming, using a mood board can help.

I often encounter clients who want to introduce colour into their homes and think that a single wall painted or papered in a bold colour or wild pattern will suffice. I suggest they opt for a more subdued colour or a simpler wallpaper and paint, or **wallpaper all the walls** in the room instead. For me, a single wall feels a bit timid and somewhat disjointed.

Finally, it's worth mentioning that many wallpaper designs are also available as fabric. Once the designer has created the pattern, it can be applied to both wallpaper and textiles. This offers numerous opportunities for stylish decoration with **matching wallpaper and fabric**, with the latter suitable for curtains, cushions, bedspreads, headboards, or upholstered furniture (depending on the fabric type), as well as shower curtains or lampshades. You can use them within the same room or have wallpaper in one room and matching textiles in another to create a harmonious connection (see Island Delight, p.70).

3

COASTAL CALMNESS

In 1912, my great-grandfather purchased a plot of land measuring about five acres along Nordstrand and the Kattegat at Nyrup Bay, the north-facing bay nestled between Klintebjerg and Rørvig in Odsherred. The farmer who subdivided the outer lots by the beach struggled to cultivate the sandy soil, and when the municipality allowed the division of land for summer houses back in the 1910s, several of the town's prominent citizens seized the opportunity.

My great-grandparents built a small bathing hut among the dunes on their newly acquired land and often rode their bikes out to enjoy afternoon coffee and a swim. City folk chuckled and shook their heads—what would one do with such a patch of sand? Anyone could just cycle down to the beach whenever they wanted. I find myself sending loving thoughts to my great-grandparents almost daily. If only they knew the joy this place has brought to me and my entire family throughout our lives.

MOOD BOARD

The watery aquamarine hues are perfectly suited for a coastal home, and in my summer house by Nordstrand, I've embraced these very shades. The vibrant floral fabric on the cushions and pouf contrasts beautifully with the solid-coloured textiles, capturing all the colours found in nature right outside our windows. The bright and faded greens, delicate aqua, sandy tones, and blues represent the old fir trees, meadows, the sea, the beach, and the sky—elements I absolutely adore. It was my mother who insisted on incorporating some colour into the house, and she was absolutely right.

The colours in the Carnival fabric from Christopher Farr provide a foundation for the home's overall colour palette. The sofa is upholstered in sand-coloured fabric, the cushions of the daybed are covered in a soft aqua linen, and the pillows are a mix of the patterned fabric and a solid light blue linen. I've also used the same fabric for curtains in front of the wardrobe. Various wool throws in sandy and aqua tones are scattered around, while an old woven rug with stripes in sea blue and beige adorns the floor. Above the dining table, blue sea-coloured pendants hang, and on the wall above the sofa is a piece created by my sister-in-law, Helene Blanche, painted by hand with ink on silk—a symbol for me of the view over the dunes towards the water during the blue hour.

The walls are painted nearly white, while the kitchen is a soft and very light blue. This is contrasted by black leather on the butterfly chair, a black table, black dining chairs, and the black cabinetry framing both the bay window and kitchen elements, including the large shelving unit for dinnerware above the kitchen counter. The tableware I've chosen consists of vibrant green and soft light green pieces—a newer set from Rosendahl and an older one from Aluminia that I collected and purchased at antique markets across the country.

THE CHERISHING OF AN IRREPLACEABLE SUMMER HOUSE

My great-grandparents had only one child, my grandmother. In 1928, my great-grandfather Vilhelm Stæhr died in a car accident. He collided with a man whose surname was Ravn, and the article about the accident in the newspaper was titled 'When Stæhr Met the Raven'.

My grandmother married my grandfather, Henning Martensen-Larsen, who was a forest ranger in Dyrehaven near Klampenborg. In 1950, my grandmother inherited the summer house, and around the same time, my grandfather got a job as a forest ranger for the royal forests around Graasten Castle in Sønderborg, where he moved with his wife and four children. My father was their youngest son. My grandparents spent many holidays at Nordstrand in Odsherred and gradually expanded the small bathing house into a larger summer house.

In the early 1960s, my grandmother passed away first, followed shortly by my grandfather. My father and his siblings inherited the land. The eldest sibling was bought out since she had moved to Norway, and the other three siblings divided the land into three equal parts. My parents built their own new summer house on their third. At the time, my mother was a recently graduated interior designer, and it was her dream to design and build it herself.

In 1967, the year I was born, the summer house was completed. The house was named Stærekassen after my great-grandfather. Throughout my upbringing, I visited this place during all holidays from Easter to autumn. I have the most amazing childhood memories of playing and swimming from morning until evening, my brother and I along with our many cousins. In the evenings, we shared meals with each other and fell asleep to the sound of the adults in the living room playing bridge—a game I also learned at a young age from my parents, and which has since become my great passion.

I have also had the opportunity to give my children the same wonderful childhood, as my mother began a generational shift many years ago. My father passed away in 1994, and my mother could no longer manage the house and land on her own. So I have now taken over the old summer house, and since the plot was fortunately large enough, it could be subdivided so that my brother and his family could also have their own summer house.

I often think about how fortunate our family is to still own this place. There have been many moments along the way where things could have turned out differently. It was, first of all, fortunate that my great-grandfather bought that sandy piece of land and didn't mind the other city dwellers laughing at him. It was fortunate that my great-grandparents only had one child. It was fortunate that my grandmother and grandfather did not sell the land during their lifetime because the distance between Sønderborg and Nykøbing Sjælland was too great; it would have been a day's journey back in the 1950s. And it was fortunate that my father and his siblings could agree to divide it into three parts, and that none of them have sold their share. Besides the beautiful location, it is the sense of community and togetherness that makes this place truly unique for our family.

No one in the family can imagine selling it. It is simply the last thing we would want to part with because it is completely irreplaceable. I see it as a place borrowed for as long as we live, but it should be passed down to our descendants. If my great-grandfather could see the truly unique gift he has passed down to his children, grandchildren, great-grandchildren, and great-great-grandchildren, I know he would be immensely happy.

Denne dag, et liv

Henrik Falk and Katrine Martensen-Larsen

In the years I have owned the house, I have lovingly cared for it, and when I met a wonderful boyfriend a couple of years ago—who happens to be the most skilled carpenter I know and is now also my business partner—we were able to give the house a tremendous lift together. Henrik builds, and we design along the way.

Most recently, Stærekassen has received the most beautiful new hand-painted kitchen. The over-moulding is constructed like a large piece of furniture and can accommodate all the glasses, cups, dishes, chopping boards, baskets, and place mats. It is designed and built specifically to fit what it needs to hold. These are the kinds of details you can obsess over when you can build it yourself.

During the construction process, we sat on the floor next to the large window facing the water, discussing how best to create a kitchen that is aligned with the house's original architectural details. Suddenly, Henrik said, "Why on earth don't we extend out towards the water with a large bay window?" The next day, he went to the timber yard and bought beams and boards to tackle yet another project. Stærekassen has truly benefitted from Henrik's expertise.

URTEGAARDEN
Argan serum
ØKO

"I believe that colours, textures, patterns, and their beauty tell stories about us, how we live, and how they impact us. This includes the colours in a room, a piece of art, decorative colourful wallpaper, and printed fabric used decoratively in a space. Colours can nourish our senses and feelings, uplift us and our creativity, and positively impact the good life."

–

Helene Blanche (1977), Danish Artist, Wallpaper and Textile Designer

INTERMEZZO

Soft furnishings

When assessing people's interior design skills, the area of soft furnishings is revealing. While it may not be the most expensive aspect of decorating, it is a **crucial area** where you can make a significant impact and complete your aesthetic. If you lack cushions, throws, curtains, or upholstered furniture, your decor is incomplete, and your home will not **exude cosiness**.

I believe it's worth investing time in selecting some beautiful **cushions and throws**, preferably in luxurious materials like wool, cashmere, linen, or velvet—textures that feel lovely when you nestle in for a nap on the sofa, and that also enhance the overall decor.

Incorporating a **variety of textures** into your interior is delightful (unlike colours, there is no limit to the number of textures you can use—more is often better). Cushions and throws made from beautiful wool or soft linen complement materials like leather, fur, rattan, canvas, and cotton—common upholstery choices for many sofas and armchairs. They also soften the harder surfaces found in your home, like wood, stone, and glass.

If you have a calm environment, using cushions and throws in a few different, complementary colours and patterns can serve as a perfect **secondary colour input**. Conversely, if your walls are lively—with lots of art or bold wallpaper—or if your sofa features a large floral or striped pattern in vivid colours, it may be wiser to select calmer, solid, or nearly solid tone-on-tone cushions and throws.

Switching out cushions and throws is also an easy way to create a **sense of change** without embarking on a larger renovation that requires contractors. New cushions and throws in a different colour palette can instantly alter the ambience of a room, all while remaining **budget friendly**. If you find yourself at a loss when choosing colours for cushions and throws, pick one or two that echo a colour in a picture or poster you have hanging in the same space.

When it comes to **upholstery and curtains**, the costs can be higher, but they are essential for achieving a cohesive interior. Upholstering one or two pieces of furniture in a patterned fabric is a perfect way to add life and personality to your home, and the pattern might even provide you with an entire colour palette (as was the case for me with the Carnival fabric from Christopher Farr in my summer house—see Coastal Calmness, p.85).

If you choose to reupholster a piece of furniture, it should have a certain quality or at least a significant sentimental value to justify the expense. Reupholstering can be costly, so it's essential to choose a **high-quality textile** and ensure that the fabric's durability is suitable for the furniture you want to upholster.

Use the mood board tool if you struggle with choosing fabrics and remember you can borrow some fabric samples from the retailer, your upholsterer, or directly from the manufacturer to evaluate them in your own space.

When it comes to curtains, you can purchase ready-made lengths in various home goods stores for very little money, or you can consult experts to have them **custom-made**. There's a vast difference in price and quality between these two approaches—much like comparing ready-made clothing to tailored garments.

If your decor is high quality, I believe you should not skimp on curtains. Certain windows can indeed be outfitted with ready-made curtains with good results, but this depends greatly on how the window opens, the depth and shape of the windowsills, and more. The cheaper alternatives simply do not suffice.

If you have windows suitable for **Roman blinds**, I cannot recommend anything other than custom-made options. I have yet to see ready-made Roman blinds in standard sizes that fit properly.

When selecting curtain fabric, I always consider how the fabric will appear from the outside. **Woven fabrics** are generally better suited than printed ones, which may have unattractive backs. I also prefer fabrics that are not too tightly woven or dark, as I love it when light can filter through. If the curtain solution needs to block out light, you may need to line the fabric or opt for separate blackout roller shades.

Just as with cushions, throws, and upholstery fabrics, select curtains in a calm fabric if your interior is already vibrant. Conversely, it can also be the curtains that introduce colour into the room; a fabric with an elegant pattern or stylish stripes can look quite luxurious.

In general, when it comes to this entire topic, you can **mix several different patterns** within the same room—as long as the colours coordinate. However, try to limit yourself to two or three colours.

4

FUNKY REFLECTIONS

In the first half of the 1970s, the British music trend that would later be dubbed glam rock emerged. It was a short form of glamour rock and a reaction against the soaring intellectualism that had developed in rock music at the end of the 1960s. I dare to draw a direct comparison from the world of music to the world of furniture and design, where we will now look at how the design duo Andrea and Rasmus Larsson, the unequivocal rock stars of the Danish interior industry, have styled their home.

MOOD BOARD

Andrea and Rasmus have transformed an old lodge on Strandvejen, just north of Copenhagen, into a solid white functionalist villa that boasts an explosion of form and colour inside. They expertly demonstrate how to decorate with an eclectic international style, large gestures, and without being beholden to Danish furniture and design traditions.

Together, they have created a multi-level villa featuring floating internal staircases, massive wooden floors, primarily white walls, and a streamlined kitchen crafted from stained oak with light Corian and marble countertops. However, this is where the classic Nordic influence completely stops, as the decor is infused with an enormous dose of glamour and sparkle.

Lavishly, the home is filled with art and books, as well as furniture and design in exotic shapes and materials like brass and green marble. There is a playful use of wild mosaics and mirrors, geometric patterns on cushions and rugs, lacquer and velvet in deep tones, as well as pastel-coloured glass and crystals. The couple experiments with bold and unconventional colour combinations such as curry yellow and burgundy, as well as royal blue and bottle green.

Anything less than extravagant would have been surprising, especially if you know even just a little about the creative design universe of the couple—Rasmus' Design By Us and Andrea's Reflections Copenhagen.

AN INTERFLOW OF COLOURS AND SHAPES

I have set out to explore the wonderful and unpretentious style universe of this couple, as it is as far removed from my own as you can get. So, where does it come from?

Rasmus, who graduated from the Danish Design School in Copenhagen, established himself as a freelancer right after finishing his education. Starting his own design firm had always been on the cards for him. His father, who was originally trained as a blacksmith, started a company that produced hospital furniture, so the household was always experimenting with fun little things and steel furniture. For Rasmus, finding a harmonious blend of design and functionality felt like playing when he was young. His mother, on the other hand, adored colours and whimsy and was always up for anything. The sense of colour must come from her, while the design enthusiasm stems from his father, Rasmus explains.

Andrea launched her company, Reflections Copenhagen, back in 2014, but in addition to being a designer, she has an extensive range of interior-related titles on her business card. Among other things, she has been an expert on various home improvement shows, authored a design book focused on wallpaper, and created several interiors for both businesses and private clients. Like Rasmus, Andrea was immersed in aesthetics and design from a young age. Her mother is a trained architect, so she grew up in an architect-designed house—albeit a wildly cosy and decorated one, she shares. "My mother was extremely skilled at combining colours and items, so I definitely inherited my slightly quirky and offbeat style from her."

I ask the couple to describe their interior style and what inspires them decoratively. Andrea begins:

"I actually think we clutter a lot—and in reality, we are totally directionless. We embrace randomness and are guided by our whims. We're not very deliberate, which is evident in many places. We don't have a specific style, but we are probably fairly modern, steering clear of the light Nordic aesthetic. We like that style in general, but we just can't figure out how to live in it. We need something that is crazier, more colourful, and wilder."

Buildings, old porcelain, art, colours, patterns, and travels are some of the inspirations Andrea draws from. Sometimes she wanders around with loose ideas, like when she wanted to create an 'Eye of the Tiger' mirror. Suddenly, she began seeing eyes everywhere. For some reason, it is primarily colour that fills her thoughts. She loves colours, especially the combination of colours. Rasmus, on the other hand, keeps an eye on everything with shapes—a hole in a wall, a building, a glass, an old ceiling, a half-finished drawing, a broken vase. He is always on the go, looking inquisitively at everything he encounters along the way.

When it comes to who has the final say in decorating their shared home, they can't provide a clear answer. They both share that responsibility. "We don't take our own decorating too seriously. It should be a home that accommodates children and young people and all their friends as well as ours. And you don't need to take your shoes off. Our approach to decorating is that if one of us wants something, we just do it. If someone takes the initiative, then 'be my guest'. We also try things out in relation to our own designs, especially Rasmus with lamp styles or something similar. The worst is when I'm fond of something; I might come home, and suddenly the lamp or dining table is gone or replaced because Rasmus has used it for a decoration or wanted to try something different."

To achieve the optimal decor, Andrea finds it essential to experiment with both colours and materials and to use freely from the palette she loves. She talks about how simply moving her accessories around can create change in an instant. Curtains and mirrors are particularly important to her. "I love curtains—they create cosiness, add colour, and can look incredibly modern and chic. Curtains give shape to the room and tie everything together," she explains, continuing: "Last but not least, there are mirrors. There's a reason I create them. They create reflections and light and can add something incredibly interesting to a room. I use them in unconventional ways, not just in hallways or bathrooms."

Perhaps Rasmus and Andrea believe that they are directionless and that their home is randomly furnished. I applaud and thank them for their glamorous and fully realised rock star style. It is well done and refreshingly different.

BEST OF
OVER&OVER
PLOP

WHAT A BEAUTIFUL WASTE OF TALENT

Andrea and Rasmus Larsson

Andrea was educated at Blaagaard Statseminarium and is also self-taught. Rasmus graduated from the Danish Design School. They each run their own company but are neighbours in an industrial district in Copenhagen Northwest.

Reflections Copenhagen was established in 2014. The company works with handmade interior accessories such as crystal table decorations, porcelain, and decorative mirrors. Andrea breaks away from the typical Scandinavian style and aims to be independent of time and place. Designs are created based on a philosophy that discourages overproduction and asserts that each design should have a valid purpose. Inspiration is clearly drawn from previous eras and design movements, with the ambition of shaping classic crystal in a new, sleek, and modern way. The fine crystal is meant to be functional and not merely a decorative object as it has traditionally been.

Design By Us was founded in 1998 by designer and TV host Rasmus Larsson. The company is built around a creative environment where design is approached under the title 'Fashion & Fantasy'. What distinguishes Design By Us is that it is not a typical Scandinavian design firm—the profile is international, bold, colourful, and eye-catching.

“Art is such a broad field. If you cut a colour open, it consists of three things: the hue it has, how light or dark it is, and how cool or warm it is. To paint is to move colours in a direction. I pull the colours in a direction, in a story, and in a universe.”

–

Tal R (1967), Danish Painter

INTERMEZZO

Art and crafts

Acquire as much **unique art and crafts** throughout your life as you can. It is through these treasures that you create a personal home, setting yourself apart from mainstream interior design. No matter how expensive your furniture, exclusive kitchens, and beautiful curtains may be, anyone can buy the same items. However, your collection of art and crafts cannot be replicated, and it **reveals who you are**. Entering a home where you can feel and see the personality of its inhabitants is, for me, one of the most inspiring experiences.

But what exactly is art? It is not just wall-hung images, oil paintings on canvas, watercolours on paper, framed prints, photographs, and sketches in pencil, chalk, or charcoal. It encompasses so much more: wooden objects, sculptures in plaster or stone, collages of paper and fabric, works made from plant fibres, mobiles, ceramics, tapestries, and figures crafted from porcelain, iron, bronze, resin, or an entirely different material. There are no limits, except that it must be **unique, handmade, and impactful**. (See Colour Extravaganza, p.42-43 and African Vibes, p.224-225)

When these unique elements enter your home, they can significantly transform your colour palette. Imagine living with white walls, white woodwork, neutral light furniture, and solid-coloured sheer curtains, and then hanging expressive art **in vibrant colours** on your walls. Or consider placing large, colourful ceramic floor vases and sculptures throughout your home and hanging mobiles from the ceilings. These elements will then create your colour palette.

Perhaps your art will create a **stark contrast** against the white surroundings, and it might be elegant to give the walls a soft hue. Just consider art museums around the world, which have long employed this technique: Thorvaldsen's in Copenhagen, the Rodin Museum in Paris, the Museum of Modern Art in New York, and London's National Gallery. Use some of the background colours from your artwork if you're seeking to achieve a harmonious and cohesive look.

No artist creates works based on how they fit into an interior design scheme. This is where we distinguish between art and applied art. As buyers, we have the **freedom to choose** the art and crafts that resonate with our personal spaces. Major art collectors might chuckle dismissively, not considering how a piece will fit in; they have entirely different agendas when purchasing art. Perhaps they seek to provoke thought or spark curiosity. Maybe they want to immerse themselves in something they may never fully understand. It could be a conversation starter, or they simply cannot live without that specific work by that particular artist. Perhaps it's an investment.

Personally, I don't feel the need to live with anything overly provocative; I tend to gravitate towards art in calmer colours, but in a variety of genres. I **buy art with my heart**: it must resonate with me aesthetically and pique my curiosity about what it is, why it exists, and how it was created. You must consider what is important to you. If it doesn't make you happy, curious, contemplative, or touch you in some way, it is probably not worth it.

Also, think about how you arrange your artworks in relation to one another. Interesting things can happen when you hang your pieces creatively, and you can transform a somewhat dull collection into something quite striking in an instant. When I hang art, I pay close attention to how the colours of the pieces harmonise, as well as their forms, to achieve a **balanced proportion**. (See Island Delight, p.75)

If you are curious about how to begin collecting and living with art in an exciting and harmonious way, I have written an entire book on the subject: *Living With Art – From Creator to Collector*.

5

FUTURISTIC NARNIA

Welcome inside a home where every key is played, and all senses are engaged. With a magnificent view of the King's Garden, Rosenborg Castle, and the Drill Square, home to the Danish Royal Guard, the multimedia artist Thomas Bickham has transformed an old, classic Copenhagen apartment into the interior design world's answer to Narnia.

MOOD BOARD

Thomas Bickham's choice of materials is sophisticated and extensive, creating a striking effect. Within the limited square footage, he revels in thick pile carpets, velvet, fox tails and raccoon and red fox fur, suede, gold, leather, and salmon skin. You'll find felt, coarsely woven boucle, dyed hessian fabric sourced from a Danish state prison, and long curtains made from wool and cashmere adorned with hand-embroidered names in shimmering pink, purple, and grey thread.

A welcoming sofa in coarse mustard-yellow fabric sits alongside homemade coffee tables cast in resin, featuring inserts of butterflies and enchanting root formations of wood from Bali. Other small tables made of smoked oak boast lavish crystal protrusions of quartz, amethyst, pyrite, and rock crystal. There are also sandstone, moss, and grasses, along with lamps adorned with preserved raw white skeleton leaves, dried bleached flowers, and feathers. Antique mirrors and vases, along with pots in golden alabaster, complete the scene.

In the living room, a large elderflower tree is decorated with preserved hydrangeas dipped in green fruit dye. A tall willow tree with catkins is planted in a granite birdbath in the bedroom. An old Indian door frame is backlit in colours transitioning from green to orange to pink, reflecting Thomas's whims. The entire setting is infused with a scent of purity accompanied by a gentle note of newly sprouted beech forest.

Creating this mood board has undoubtedly been the most challenging aspect of the project. Fortunately, Annette Von Einem (one of the world's most talented floral artists) advised me to spray paint a dried hydrangea instead of attempting to use fruit dye—sorry, Thomas. You probably aren't entirely pleased that my resin-cast blue morpho butterfly is only a sketch. As a consolation, I've hidden a small diamond, your favourite colour, on the board—you'll have to see if you can find it. Additionally, I've gifted you a Jacaranda flower that I personally picked, dried, and brought all the way back from Buenos Aires, Argentina. I hope you like it.

AN EXPLOSION OF IMPRESSIONS

With outstretched arms and the warmest smile, I am welcomed. Thomas is a true bon vivant. But it's not just his heartfelt hospitality that leaves me in awe; my senses are already on high alert. As I ascend the stairs, muted classical music wafts towards me from the open door on the third floor. I love it when people throw their front doors wide open; it speaks volumes about their desire to engage with the world and meet new people.

It's not only the music that flows freely from the open door; I'm also greeted by an inviting scent of freshness mixed with a gentle note of newly sprouted beech forest. At first, I only register the fragrance subconsciously, and perhaps that's why it feels so delicate.

Before Thomas emerges from the back of the apartment, I notice that my sense of sight is now working overtime. The initial impressions have been so overwhelming that I struggle to maintain eye contact. Thomas is unfazed by my wandering gaze—he's clearly used to it.

The extravagant trees and branches adorned with feathers, flowers, and leaves immediately capture my attention. Some hang from the ceiling, while others stand in large, beautiful vases and pots in corners and on dressers. In several places, they are even wrapped around lamps.

The walls are painted in subdued matte greys, warm greens, and beige earth tones, while a large old door from an Indian temple leans casually against the wall in the living room. Here also hangs the artwork *Dead Artists Don't Make Any Money* by Klaus Köenig, while the other explosive artworks—all created by Thomas himself—testify to his immense imagination and creativity. One piece features flowers and branches spilling forth from a bare canvas, and above the sofa hang two round mirrors with decorative embellishments. Those are 'yes-hat' artworks, Thomas explains, adding that if you stand beneath one and take a selfie, you can say 'yes' to everything for the rest of the day.

In the dining room, there is a self-portrait. At first glance, it appears to be a nearly blank piece of glass, but then you catch sight of the dandelion that has shed all its seeds to the wind, with only one flying against the current. You only need to know Thomas for a couple of minutes to understand its significance.

In the kitchen, Thomas showcases the left and right hemispheres of his brain. Unsurprisingly, the right one is a jumble of creativity, accented by a tiny touch of his favourite colour. Diamond, of course—what else?

The furniture is inviting; the plump mustard-yellow sofa is utterly irresistible, while the poufs made of fox tails lounge along the floor, and the intricate details on the sophisticated tables—wood formations cast in resin or preserved forest floor moss—evoke images of woods and lakes, trolls, witches, and other supernatural beings. The only piece Thomas hasn't made himself is the sofa, and everything else can be ordered from him.

The lighting in the apartment can, of course, change to all sorts of colours, designed to match the various moods Thomas wants to create. The large, soft, fluffy rugs are the finishing touch to a complete and entirely enchanting decor. Thomas's place is so visually striking that the rooms resonate deeply. It's an explosion of impressions, and yes—standing here in the midst of it all—one must conclude that, even though the apartment likely offers one of the most beautiful views in Copenhagen, Thomas has made the view of Rosenborg Castle almost redundant with his magic.

Before I leave, I am invited to embroider my name into a curtain length in the dining room. It's his guest curtain book, and I can choose to stitch with pink, purple, or grey silk thread. Of course, nothing here is like it is for the rest of us.

Thomas Bickham

Thomas Bickham originally trained as a clothing operator. He has worked as a hosiery model, hairdresser, make-up artist, drag queen, singer, songwriter, event creator, stylist, and designer. For the past 20 years, he has created furniture and lamps as well as lavish floral arrangements for private and commercial clients. In Denmark, most people know him as the main designer from the TV programme ***De Fantastiske Fem***, where he successfully transformed ordinary Danish homes into magical spaces.

Since the photos in his Copenhagen apartment were taken, Thomas has moved to Marbella, Spain, where he is developing new ways of living that connect people with themselves, each other, and nature through regenerative principles, neuroarchitecture, art, and spirituality.

"I have spent my whole life studying the colours in nature, and there is still so much to learn."

–

Claude Monet (1840-1926), French Painter

INTERMEZZO

Plants and flowers

At Thomas Bickham's place, we observe how flowers and plants are transformed into genuine works of art. But don't worry—less can certainly be more. Green plants and flowers, whether **fresh, cut, preserved, dried, or artificial**, can all infuse colour into your decor and bring it to life. Personally, I have a fondness for dried flowers, and if I do choose artificial ones, I decidedly prefer those made from paper or felt rather than plastic.

Nature is my greatest **source of inspiration**, where I gather ideas on how to use flowers and branches for decor. Springtime is enchanting as everything begins to bloom, but there's a specific magic in autumn when nature starts to fade, and even in winter when everything is completely dried up. Every year, before the frost sets in, I diligently prune my hydrangeas from the garden and let them dry indoors. I love the muted aesthetic of the blooms once the colours have faded (see Scandic Oriental, p.196). I keep them displayed year-round, and during holidays like Christmas and New Year, I may add a touch of gold or silver to make them festive.

In my summer house, **dried reeds, rushes, and grasses** are among my favourites, particularly those I gather along the coast. A large bouquet of fresh-cut flowers can be absolutely wonderful, but their lifespan is short, and the water needs to be changed daily, especially if they're in a clear glass vase. I'd rather do without a bouquet standing in murky, foul-smelling water. Similarly, if the bouquet has been bought at a petrol station, it's a definite pass for me, and this has nothing to do with the price. Cute little potted plants and ostentatious poinsettias in overly decorated flowerpots are also a no-go in my home; these are among the first things I remove when helping clients achieve a successful decor.

From a particularly knowledgeable friend, I've learned that using the same floral arrangements year-round can make them feel dull. There's something cosy about looking forward to the arrival of flowers from each new season. He also taught me the technique of **arranging bouquets** directly in the vase, rather than tying them together. This approach affords greater freedom and lends a more relaxed, spontaneous look to the arrangement. And remember, the vase is just as essential as the flowers. A **beautiful vase** doesn't require much; even a few select flowers or a sculptural branch can create an impressive display. (See Scandic Oriental, p.192 and Pastel Elegance, p.246-255)

I can't claim to have green fingers, and perhaps that's why dried bouquets work so well for me. I wish I had the knack for managing **large pots of green plants**, and I envy those who can nurture a big fig tree, monstera, or lemon tree (see Scandic Oriental, p.198-199). If, like me, you struggle to keep plants alive, it can be a good idea to use companies that can both deliver and care for your plants. Large plants are expensive, and when they look half-wilted, they contribute little in terms of colour, atmosphere, or joy. If you have many plants, it's best to stick to **uniform, monochromatic pots**; otherwise, the display can quickly become a chaotic jumble that detracts from what truly matters—the beauty of the plants themselves.

Ultimately, whether through dried florals or vibrant greens, integrating flowers and plants into your home decor can create a dynamic and inviting atmosphere. They can **evoke emotions**, remind us of nature, and offer a personal touch that reflects our individual style.

6

COUNTRY AMBIENCE

A copy of a copy of a barn. It sounds strange, but it's true. On about two acres of land in North Zealand, Mette and Mikkel Adsbøl have built yet another barn to frame their family and work life. Unlike their previous barn, which was whitewashed and topped with red tiles, this one is clad in cedar wood with steel roofing and sharp, clean lines..

From a distance, the building appears relatively modest, nestled in the landscape as it overlooks fields and meadows. However, as you approach the entrance, you are greeted by an impressive double main door, handcrafted from solid oak. The closer you get, the more the door's details come into focus—carvings that form a sun shape, referencing the way sunlight breaks through the forest edge at dawn. This humility is clearly no longer present.

MOOD BOARD

The tones within the home are calm, primarily consisting of wood, wood, and more wood. There are planks on the floor; wide, raw, untreated, and whitewashed pine boards on the ceilings; and visible beams that form the house's structure. The kitchen fronts and island are made of oak, and both the dining table and coffee table are crafted from wood—oak, smoked oak, and teak—while the chairs feature woven seats.

The few wall sections remaining after the large windows and door areas have claimed much of the vertical space are painted in muted, dusty grey-green tones. Long, raw white silk curtains with loosely woven vertical stripes delicately match the wall colour.

'But there's no colour here,' some might think. I couldn't disagree more. There are plenty of tones, just no bright or bold colours, except for the green plants and the green pattern woven into the rug under the coffee table. By the way, Mette personally imports the rugs, woven from wool with the most exquisite long pile, from Morocco. Greyish tones are echoed in the upholstery of the furniture—cotton velvet on the sofa and sheepskin on 'The Tired Man', Mogens Lassen's world-renowned armchair.

And of course, let's not forget the guest bathroom, painted in a wild and vibrant arsenic green, and the master bedroom, where the grey-green hue is intensified on both the walls and ceiling, making the atmosphere more intimate, while the cabinets are painted a delectable chocolate brown. In the adjoining bathroom, an old dresser is painted in a lovely dusty green colour and transformed into a sink cabinet, while the chocolate brown colour is repeated on the frame.

I notice that not a single surface in the decor is white. Only the small glass elements in the chandeliers are white—and that's just during the day, for when darkness falls and the lights are turned on, they glow like tiny suns in a warm yellow tone. The subdued colours also come from the many accessories, lamps, and curtain rods in brass, as well as the mustard-yellow Moroccan ceramic plates on the wall and the bold candlesticks scattered around the home with a carefree touch. Dark blue and green tones are also hidden in the storm-patterned cushions sewn for the built-in bench along the enormous window area in the gable.

CHOICES THAT LAST A LIFETIME

To get closer to nature, Mette and Mikkel Adsbøl built their dream house not far from here about ten years ago. A whitewashed barn with a red tiled roof. They were tired of forest excursions feeling like a burdensome weekend project and wanted to live in the midst of nature. Their boys should grow up surrounded by open spaces and picturesque views of fields, and learn how to drive a tractor, just as they did when they were growing up.

"We both love old details and items with patina, and we never thought we would build and live in a new house, but we simply couldn't find anything old that met our requirements," Mikkel explains.

The new house resembles an old barn because, earlier in the process, the couple had considered a plot where there was indeed an old barn that could be renovated. Before the municipality decided that the residential area would be too large and the project fell through, the couple had already designed and renovated the barn down to the smallest detail—at least on paper.

"We were so excited about that barn and the layout we had devised, with the potential for an extremely high ceiling and a very unique room configuration, that we decided to build exactly that," Mikkel clarifies.

Mette and Mikkel loved their newly built home but dreamed of having even more distance from their neighbours. When the opportunity arose to purchase the perfect plot of land, they jumped at the chance to start over. They wanted to build another barn, maintaining a similar internal structure, but this time with a bit more square footage and in wood, as they sought a more organic and streamlined expression.

To make the finances work, the couple hired a skilled carpenter, and Mikkel personally assisted throughout the construction phase. After two years of blood, sweat, and tears, in 2023 the family could celebrate their first Christmas in the new barn, a home where everything is now refined down to the smallest detail. Let me attempt to describe how I experienced it.

Upon entering through the front door, you step onto large marble slabs with an elegant cross pattern inlaid with brass strips. The symmetrically placed large wardrobes with curved fronts frame the hall while towering up to the apex. The ceiling is so surprisingly high that your eyes widen, making it impossible to maintain eye contact with Mikkel, who welcomes you.

Two long axes run through the house: one leading to the bedrooms and bathrooms, while the other goes from the hall directly to the kitchen and living area. This gigantic space features a kitchen with tall cabinets and a cooking section along the end wall, facing a massive floating island. There's subsequently a large area dedicated to the dining space, beautifully marked by a stone-clad chimney and an integrated wood stove, with wide doorways leading to the outdoor areas to both the east and west. Most striking is the entire visible roof structure, where raw, untreated, and whitewashed pine boards have replaced typical drywall.

At the far end of the room, a couple of steps lead up to the back half of the expansive room, which measures over 150 square metres. The change in level was a clever design choice, marking zones and adding visual interest. Although the ceiling remains over six metres high as you step into the living room, it feels a bit more intimate and cosier in this section. The elevated level also offers a formidable view over the landscape as far as the eye can see.

In the decor, Mette has prioritised wood, stone, and muted Nordic colours, boldly combining Danish design classics with rugs and accessories sourced from Morocco, as well as international textiles from Italian Dedar, among others. Mette swears by long-lasting solutions and doesn't focus much on current trends. She chooses with her heart and can quickly sense if something is right or wrong.

"I always prioritise materials and quality, preferably handcrafted, that will last forever and only get more beautiful with time," she concludes.

Mette and Mikkel Beck Adsbøl

Mette Beck Adsbøl works as a self-employed home and interior stylist. Together with her husband, photographer Mikkel Beck Adsbøl, she has travelled extensively in Morocco, particularly in Marrakech, where she initially sought unique interior pieces for her own decor. In doing so, she encountered a range of skilled local artisans and quickly recognised the potential for some of the items she had produced to be sold to prospective clients in Denmark—and not least, to be used in her own interior projects. With her special ability to see what minor adjustments are needed for Moroccan products to work in harmony with Nordic interior design, it didn't take long for Mette to design her own line of Berber rugs, ceramics, and accessories.

Mikkel is one of Denmark's most celebrated food and interior photographers. He has contributed his talent to numerous cookbooks and interior design publications, including several images featured in this book. In addition to his photography skills, Mikkel is quite handy and has played an active role in constructing his new home.

"I believe that if you are aware of the colours in your environment, you can affect the atmosphere around you."

–

Olafur Eilasson (1967), Danish-Icelandic Artist

INTERMEZZO

Wood, stone and tiles

You may not immediately associate materials like wood and stone with colour in interior design. However, everyone agrees that tiles, which come **in a myriad of colours**, patterns, and shapes, can add a significant splash to a decor.

In a kitchen, tiles behind the cooking area and sink can be the impactful element that introduces bold hues into the room. Perhaps you dream of an olive-green bathroom and are considering installing coloured tiles. If you do, I recommend painting the walls white. Alternatively, you could paint the walls olive green (and possibly the ceiling) and opt for neutral tiles. It's essential to think carefully before choosing to install **coloured and patterned tiles** (see Funky Reflections, p.125). This choice can be a trend, and it's generally easier and cheaper to repaint (or change towels and shower curtains) than to replace tiles.

We often think of stone as being in natural colours, but in recent years, we've seen quite a bit of **marble in colours** such as pink or green, especially on countertops. This can be a lovely way to introduce some colour. But what about stones in neutral tones? Travertine or granite used on walls or floors can also contribute colour and atmosphere. The stone may be grey-brown, beige, cream, or nearly black, but it still adds a hue that will influence the ambience of the space.

And what about wood? Do you think of **wood as a colour**? I certainly do—and I'm sure you've considered at some point that a pine dresser can appear too yellowish, a cherry wood floor too reddish, or a cabinet with wenge fronts too brown. This evidence shows that we perceive wood as coloured, and therefore we need to pay attention to wood types when planning our palette.

Wood types can also be a trend phenomenon, so **think carefully** about which wood species you choose if you plan to invest in new wooden floors for your home. It's a costly investment and not something you can easily change. Floors (and tiles) are elements that prospective buyers notice. If the flooring suits their taste, you'll likely recoup your investment—or even better.

In general, the more **uniform and beautiful** your flooring is, the more harmonious your decor will appear. While it can be exciting to change colours from room to room, having different floors in each space is inadvisable. You can have the most beautiful furniture, but if your flooring is disappointing, your decor will never reach its full potential. Conversely, you could live in a cardboard box with a beautiful floor and be happy.

Wood is also frequently used for cabinet fronts and furniture. Therefore, it's essential to be mindful when integrating wood into your decor. In fact, you can never have too much of this beautiful, organic, living, and **highly durable material**. First and foremost, consider the type of wood, and then also think about the treatment your wood has received or will require.

The colour of the wood can vary significantly depending on whether it's smoked (which darkens it), soap-treated (which gives it a milky white hue), or oiled (which can make it golden or tinted if the oil is coloured). Furthermore, hardwoods like ash and oak will turn grey over time if left untreated.

Stripping old doors or furniture will also alter the colour of the item. The **stripping process** will lighten the wood, which can then be treated with lye if you want to prevent it from yellowing again. Afterwards, you'll need to consider the finish, such as soap, lacquer, or oil. This entire area concerning wood types, treatments, and their behaviours is almost a science, so always seek professional advice.

When choosing a wood type for a new piece of furniture, I often recommend selecting the same type as your flooring or other fixed elements in your home that you appreciate. Oak, walnut, and teak are, in my opinion, beautiful wood types, and you can certainly mix them. Interestingly, it can be very successful to **blend a wide variety of wood** types, especially if all other tones in the decor are neutral—beige, cream, linen, nearly white, and greyish. However, if you mix a multitude of wood types, their finishes, and incorporate a mix of strong colours, there's a significant risk that the overall expression may become chaotic.

7

SCANDIC ORIENTAL

In the heart of Odense, Denmark's third-largest city, stands a large, solid manor house. Designed and constructed according to all the rules of art at the end of the 19th century, it features red bricks with decorative headers above the windows, a slate roof, copper gutters, and a prominent white cornice band beneath the eaves, beautifully highlighting the carvings in the roof structure's gable ends.

In the house on Allégade, Maria and Joakim Løth have decorated the ground floor—over 200 beautiful square metres with high ceilings, en-suite living rooms, parquet floors, divided-light windows, stucco, and high panels. Additionally, they renovated the old garage in the back garden and moved in their interior design business.

MOOD BOARD

Inside, as well as outside, the architects have meticulously attended to the details. The floor boasts wide planks arranged in a stunning herringbone pattern, while the walls and ceilings are adorned with panels, mouldings, and the finest stucco work.

The overall colour palette in the interior is calm, featuring off-white walls and panels throughout every room. This soft contrast beautifully complements the rustic wooden furniture, which is expertly paired with plush, voluminous dining chairs upholstered in cognac-coloured leather, light grey sheepskin lounge chairs, and a cream wool sofa. The crowning jewels of the home are the elegant glass chandeliers that add a touch of sophistication.

The colour scheme is inspired by the striking artworks of Sabina Von Essen, which hang in the dining room and living area. The various oriental rugs in faded shades of orange, pink, ochre, beige, brown, sand, soft green, and light blue have been carefully selected to harmonise with the artwork. A wealth of green plants in terracotta pots provides a noticeable contrast to the otherwise delicate and subdued palette.

Although there is a significant difference in the patterns and origins of Persian and Indian rugs—some made from silk and others from wool—they share a cohesive style that allows them to function beautifully together in the space. As you look through the rooms, from one rug to the next, there is a common thread that connects them all. And that thread is present throughout, creating a seamless flow and a genuinely inviting atmosphere.

NORDIC WITH A HINT OF PERSIA

With grand gestures, the architect set to work at the drawing board back in the 1870s. He could trust that the mason, carpenter, and joiner were skilled in their crafts, as the level of detail in the masonry and woodwork is rare and exquisitely executed.

Note how a decorative carving in the gable's verge allows the French balcony door to have an unobstructed view. Originally, you could gaze far across the fields and meadows from this vantage point, but over the years, the villa has witnessed the city encroaching. Today, Allégade lies almost in the centre of Odense, and the grandeur of life—complete with a cook and kitchen in the basement, maids in the attic, and two Rolls Royces in the garage—has long since changed.

Ten years ago, Maria and Joakim purchased the property, which had functioned for years as a course facility associated with a nearby school. Here, they were able to realise their dream and run their business. Joakim, who originally owned a custom carpentry business, changed direction a few years ago and now runs a large company producing and selling solid oak furniture, which the couple designs themselves.

Joakim crafts his furniture from French wine presses that have been in use for years, exuding history. The pieces are rustic, raw, and robust with their inviting scent of wood. The surfaces are luxuriously soft, and the quality is unmistakable—as is the weight.

The couple are right in their assertion that a piece of furniture tells a story about the person who chose it. I agree with them that when you welcome guests into your home, office, or wherever the furniture is located, it narrates the story of someone who values quality, exclusivity, skilled craftsmanship, and sustainability.

Joakim is committed to ensuring that his furniture retains its value, gains significant sentimental worth, and ultimately becomes the new heirloom of families. I wholeheartedly support him, as very few pieces produced today can withstand the test of generations.

In addition to defining zones, such as the dining area or sofa group, Maria and Joakim demonstrate that an oriental rug can possess just as much personality as a piece of furniture. Rugs are not merely functional; for example, in their hall lies a Persian silk rug—the finest you can find and a work of art in itself. The rug is signed by the creator and changes colour dramatically depending on the angle from which it is viewed.

Surrounding the large, sturdy dining table—also crafted by Joakim from old French oak wine presses—are comfortable upholstered dining chairs, and above the table hang modern glass chandeliers. Behind the dining table is artwork by Swedish contemporary artist Sabina Von Essen, and under the table lies a vintage Persian Kerman rug. This rug was chosen to harmonise with the style and colours of the chairs and artwork. In the kitchen, Maria and Joakim selected a vintage patchwork runner that matches the dining table rug in both style and tones.

In the office, there's a Ziegler fine rug from Persia, made from 100% wool, and in the bedroom lies a Kashkuli rug from Persia. This is a somewhat rarer, heavier, and sturdier nomadic rug—also made of wool—with symbols inspired by Persian tales and traditions.

In the two connected living rooms, there are two Tabriz rugs from India. In front of the sofa lies a Royal rug, and by the lounge chairs is an Indi rug. Both rugs are produced with inspiration from Persian Tabriz designs and were chosen because the grand living room can accommodate a classic oriental rug. Additionally, the tables are beautifully unpretentious, while the upholstered furniture from Fogia is very contemporary. The colours here are also coordinated with the artwork above the sofa by Sabina Von Essen.

NORDIC MOODS

NORDIC MOODS

Maria and Joakim Løth

Together, Maria and Joakim Løth run the company By Løth. Joakim designs and builds rustic tables and smaller furniture from old French oak wine presses, primarily to order. Maria is a partner in the business and also works as a home stylist.

Regarding his furniture, Joakim explains that each piece is unique due to the nature, history, and distinctive patina of the wood. They are made from dried old French oak sourced from ancient wine presses, and Joakim often travels to France to select the exact presses from which he will build his furniture.

The furniture is designed to last nearly a lifetime and can withstand being placed both indoors and outdoors—even in our Nordic climate. Their style fits seamlessly in newly built homes, contrasting beautifully with the clean lines of the architecture, as well as in older buildings, where it harmonises with the character of the house.

The furniture is primarily sold through the couple's own network and on their social media platforms, such as Instagram and Facebook, to customers both domestically and internationally, under the name By Løth.

"Colours are energy! The dynamics of the colours in the sky – the slow transition between warm ochre shades and deep blue tones at dusk – create a healing sensation that fills both body and soul with happiness and gratitude."

–

Christina Augustesen (1975), Danish Artist and Lighting Designer

INTERMEZZO

Rugs

Rugs—specifically loose rugs—can serve **many functions** in a home. They can define and unite spaces, such as a seating area, home office, or dining room. They provide comfort underfoot, improve the acoustics of a room, and add decorative flair while infusing colour and ambience into the space.

A rug can also **set the tone** for your home's style. Whether you choose modern graphic patterns, Moroccan kilims, or ornate oriental designs, it's important to be cautious when mixing different rug styles, as this can quickly lead to visual chaos. Like flooring, the more uniform your rugs are throughout the home, the more harmonious the overall look will be. (See Pastel Elegance, p.248-260 and African Vibes, p.216-221)

Conversely, you can create striking contrast by blending a particular rug genre with a completely different interior style. For example, in the home of Maria and Joakim, a modern Scandinavian decor is beautifully complemented by exclusive Persian rugs. Remember, it is where contrasts meet that **interesting tension** arises.

If your walls are vibrant, or if you have a rich assortment of patterned textiles on cushions, upholstery, and curtains, or colourful and expressive artwork on the walls, opt for calm, perhaps even solid-coloured rugs (see Futuristic Narnia, p.152). Choose rugs that **focus on texture and quality** rather than bold patterns. Conversely, if your decor is very subdued, patterned rugs can be a stunning choice. This also applies to spaces that are otherwise quiet, such as a bedroom or hallway; here, you can certainly allow yourself to choose a patterned rug. (See Colour Extravaganza, p.46)

The size of the rug is crucial. The **proportions** need to fit the area where the rug will be placed. I believe a rug should not be a massive island on which the sofa, coffee table, and armchairs will sit. Instead, I prefer leaving about 10 cm of bare floor between the rug and the sofa. The rug should be about 10–20 cm wider than the length of the sofa, ensuring that the entire coffee table is on the rug while perhaps only half of the armchair(s) fits comfortably. A good rug size for a standard seating arrangement is 170x240 cm or 200x300 cm, both standard dimensions for many rugs.

For a **dining table set-up**, the rug should be longer and wider than the dining table itself, including the chairs around it. It's acceptable for the back legs of the chairs to extend onto the floor when they are pulled back. Focus instead on whether the legs can move easily across the rug without getting caught, as this may cause daily frustration for some. If your dining table is square or round, you can find rugs in those shapes; while this can look elegant, I personally prefer an elongated rug under my round dining table.

Runners along stairs or corridors also contribute to decorating 'empty' spaces and serve as effective colour generators. Ensure that the runner has the proper width; there should be a bit of space from the wall so that the floor is visible, but it shouldn't be too narrow (see Country Ambience, p.174). If you're having a custom-made runner, be meticulous in measuring and ensure that doors can open freely without catching on the rug.

8

AFRICAN VIBES

Just a 30-minute drive from Copenhagen, on a large, hilly plot with an extravagant old planting of fruit trees, rhododendrons, and a massive clematis, Birgitte Steengaard and Vagn Brandrup have constructed an exquisite example of a black-painted wooden house. Adorned with white divided-light windows, gables, and terraces, it evokes thoughts of a Danish summer house with a light Scandinavian interior style based on cool, subdued Nordic hues. However, that is far from the reality.

MOOD BOARD

Despite the fact that the walls in this home are purely white, you are greeted by a vibrant explosion of colours—lime green, ochre, burnt brown, orange, Chinese red, and olive. You can almost smell and taste the essence of the medina in Marrakech and the bazaars of Istanbul.

Dark wooden figures and masks, shamans and dream catchers, along with dried flowers and leaves adorn the space. There are feathers, hides, antlers, and a mix of chains and pitchers, as well as silver cases and emblems combined with Chinese chests and candlesticks from French churches.

The floors are covered with thick Berber rugs, reminiscent of the ancient Rya rugs, featuring the characteristic zigzag patterns in black and white tones. However, what stands out the most are the many unique kilim rugs and cushions adorned with geometric patterns, stripes, and floral designs. The home is a true treasure trove of finds and collectibles, and you are in for a delightful surprise.

Nestled among the eclectic decor, a collection of books from around the world beckons visitors to lose themselves in tales of adventure and discovery. Each shelf is a portal to different cultures and perspectives, offering a source of inspiration and insight. In the kitchen, hand-painted ceramics and artisan-crafted utensils display the owners' dedication to both function and aesthetic appeal. The aromas of spices and herbs waft from the culinary corner, enhancing the senses with hints of far-off lands.

The eclectic mix of artefacts creates an atmosphere rich in cultural narratives, inviting guests to explore and appreciate the stories behind each piece. From the bold colours to the varied textures, every corner of the home reflects a passion for travel, art, and the beauty of craftsmanship, ensuring that this space is not just a residence, but a living gallery of experiences and memories.

In the garden, vibrant Rhododendron and fragrant jasmine create a serene outdoor oasis. The blend of natural elements and artistic expressions creates a harmonious balance, inviting nature indoors and inviting the outdoors into the home.

A TREASURE CHEST FOR UNIQUE FINDS

On a large dresser in the hall, a row of stuffed birds gazes down from their protective glass domes and small yet ego-boosting displays. The birds watch over their home and its owners, while you, as a guest, are appraised. To the right of the dresser hangs a lavish, centuries-old silk dress from Istanbul beneath a richly decorated Turkish fez. It's a wild still life to welcome guests, but with a humorous demonstration of power, the tone is set.

The house, spanning a total of 340 square metres over three levels, was designed by the couple and constructed by a German contracting firm. This way, they could have it exactly as they wanted. Birgitte took charge of the interior design, while her husband focused on the broader architectural lines.

Though the atmosphere is reminiscent of the East, a generous dose of French country style is interwoven throughout. This is most evident in the dining room, with wicker chairs surrounding the old Provençal long table, and in the kitchen, where the sumptuous country stove signifies serious cooking taking place.

The ethnic colours in the decor are provided by countless kilims, cushions, and throws, as well as small artworks by Olox, Charlotte Thymark, and Søs Brysch. Additionally, all the charming and quirky items, casually scattered throughout the home, can be found on the walls, fireplace, dressers, tables, and chests, or lying in windowsills—contributing to the oriental atmosphere. Be prepared to pinch yourself to avoid getting lost in Birgitte's medina.

Masks, figurines, pitchers, boxes, emblems, costumes, dresses, feathers, dream catchers, antlers, wreaths, and chains, as well as stuffed animals—there is so much to explore that you might not know where to begin.

Birgitte has shopped in antique stores and markets both at home and abroad for years, particularly in Turkey and Morocco, which explains the myriad soulful treasures she has curated, and she has certainly cracked the code on how to live comfortably with her collection.

It's hardly interesting if all the items you've spent hours searching for, carefully wrapping, and transporting home from a trip end up hidden in a moving box, left to gather dust in an attic or basement. Birgitte compellingly demonstrates how she uses every surface to showcase her many unique finds. The items are arranged like small still lifes, elegantly placed on trays, encased in glass domes, or hung up. It may seem casual, but it is anything but.

The colours are most vibrant on the ground floor, while Birgitte experiments with a more subdued look on the first floor, featuring black and white Berber rugs with the recognisable zigzag pattern. She became fascinated by this style during a trip to Marrakech.

On the Chinese dresser placed in a corner of the spacious bedroom, an industrial lamp sits, and decoratively, large wooden rolls with gift ribbon are displayed under a glass dome, while a thick bundle of chains casually hangs from the door handle. The walls are adorned with antlers, masks, and dream catchers, and on a wooden stump in the corner stands a richly decorated Sherman figure made by Paula Viitanen. Though this space is a mix of many different styles, everything is beautifully tied together—thanks to the colours.

The Sherman figure was created by Finnish artist Paula Viitanen, who is based in Denmark, and the dream catcher was a gift to Birgitte. It is precisely these elements that make the home so personal and demonstrate that art can be much more than traditional wall decorations, such as paintings or posters.

Even in the bathroom, Birgitte has integrated her ethnic style. The elements in the room were custom-made by the couple; they purchased some old shutters, had them tailored, and then stained them dark. Additionally, the room features a large old French linen cabinet, classic brass fixtures, a lovely old basket, a wooden-framed mirror, Turkish hammam towels, and a large wooden tray for various items on the table.

Visiting homes like that of Birgitte and Vagn—with exciting collections and an interesting, artistic way of displaying objects—truly inspires me.

Living Under Glass

Birgitte Steengaard

Birgitte originally trained as a banker, but 35 years ago started a business just outside Copenhagen, specialising in down clothing. Over the years, many other product categories and items were added to her range. For the past 30 years, she has been trading in rugs, and 10 years ago, she completely ceased dealing in clothing.

Her true passion lies in rugs—primarily kilim rugs from Turkey, sourced from Turkish regions such as Sivas, Kayseri, Kars, Karabag, Konya, and Barak. Today, she has moved her showroom into her home, allowing customers to get a much better sense of how to integrate the rich oriental colours into a Nordic home.

"Colour is the key to the beauty of art; it is the means by which we can express the innermost feelings and emotions that words cannot."

–

Sir John Soane (1753-1837), British Architect and Antiquity Collector

INTERMEZZO

Collectibles

Collector's homes are the spaces that inspire me the most. These are environments where owners have diligently searched their entire lives for the perfect figurine, candlestick, bowl, pitcher, medallion, or sculpture. They have not only amassed impressive collections but also seamlessly integrated these treasures into their decor. Often, these homes are **rich in artistic expression**, though the topic of art has its own dedicated section in this book.

For me, the specific items being collected are less important than the scale of the collection and the way it is displayed. Collectibles should reside within the home, occupying their **own dedicated spaces** to provide daily joy to the owners and wonder, curiosity, and inspiration to visitors.

In addition to creating an appealing environment, collectibles—including art—serve as perfect conversation starters. They **provoke questions**: Where did the interest originate? Where were the items found? How were they created? What stories lie behind each piece? A collection adds significant character to a home, enhancing its ambience both literally and metaphorically. As a collector, you likely know the thrill of discovering the perfect addition, the thought process involved in finding its ideal place, and the satisfaction that follows when everything comes together cohesively.

Items that can be hung on walls, displayed on shelves, or arranged in open cabinets or glass-fronted cases are certainly easier to showcase than African garments, ancient texts, or Viking coins. These require more creative thinking regarding **display methods**, such as whether they can be framed, placed under glass on a coffee table, arranged as a still life, displayed in a showcase, or set up on a pedestal. (See African Vibes, p.219, 222, 224, 228)

It's undoubtedly easiest to collect items that can be used daily or for special occasions, such as beautiful vintage glassware, ceramic pitchers, a special set of silver cutlery, or an entire set of antique porcelain. Rugs from specific regions, candlesticks from French churches, or Italian glass lamps from Murano are especially easy to integrate thanks to their **functional purpose**.

However, serious collectors often don't choose what to collect based solely on the ease of living with the items. That aspect tends to resolve itself; once it does, everything beautifully falls into place. Collectors are passionate individuals who amass items that reflect their personalities, values, and experiences, and the world of collecting encompasses a **wide variety of interests**.

Motivations for collecting vary widely; some are driven by a genuine love for what they gather, often rooted in childhood memories or cultural interests, while others are captivated by the historical significance of their items, feeling a responsibility as custodians of heritage. Collecting fosters **a sense of community** as enthusiasts join clubs, attend exhibitions, and participate in online forums to share their passions.

Displaying a collection can be an art form in itself, requiring careful curation to create meaningful vignettes that enhance the visual appeal of a space. An effective display can draw attention to individual items through **strategic lighting** and complementary decor, transforming an ordinary home into a personal gallery filled with history, stories, and often colours. And actually, a collection can be colourful in more than a literal sense.

9

PASTEL ELEGANCE

For Jette Witzke, home decor should endure for many years, and her home should not be filled with fleeting trends and fads. According to her, we should invest in furniture that can last a lifetime, and she still cherishes items from when she first moved out. The old craftsmanship—which never goes out of style—is her mantra. Together with her husband Kim, she has beautifully renovated a large classic manor villa just north of Copenhagen.

MOOD BOARD

Soft pink, burnt brown, watery blue-green, and a touch of yellow and orange are the primary ingredients in Jette Witzke's colour palette, set against a neutral linen background. These muted tones can be found in the faded, beautiful antique kilim rugs that adorn the large living rooms and spacious bedrooms, dictating the colour palette for the rest of the furnishings throughout the house.

Throughout the home, the carefully curated decor not only illustrates Jette's artistic vision but also turns each room into a narrative space filled with warmth, character, and an unmistakable sense of style. The coarsely woven kilim rugs are beautifully complemented by upholstered sofas, daybeds, armchairs, and poufs, along with an abundance of throws and cushions made solely from velvet and linen. Given the intricate patterns of the kilim rugs, it's a wise choice to keep all other textiles in solid colours. Large glass vases filled with blooming country roses from the garden adorn tables and dressers.

The excitement in the decor arises from the interplay between the antique and the modern, evident in every room. This contrast is most pronounced in the living room, where the chandelier and the oval portraits from the Golden Age bring history to a sleek, modern sofa group and a lively bookshelf.

It is also present in the kitchen, where old jars add character to the otherwise minimalistic kitchen elements, and in the bathroom, where antique mirrors and the chandelier create a cosy atmosphere in what would otherwise be a clinical space.

This balance of old and new serves as a tribute to timeless elegance and personal expression, making every visit a unique experience in this captivating environment.

FRANSKE FORBINDELSER
FRANSKE FORBINDELSER
THE PARIS RITZ

HAND-MIXED HUES FOR ADDED WARMTH

In addition to ensuring that the age of the house aligns with the items used for decoration, the colours within the home are of utmost importance to Jette. She speaks about the particular tranquillity that arises when there are consistent tones flowing from room to room. This resonates deeply with me. Art, furniture, rugs, and wall colours must work together in a cohesive colour palette, and in the classic large manor villa just outside Copenhagen, she convincingly demonstrates how this can be achieved.

Old kilim rugs are perfect for unifying colours within a room, and Jette prefers those with age and patina, as their faded tones contribute to a soft colour scheme. In one of the living rooms, a large, fully stocked, custom-built bookshelf stands proudly—Jette cannot imagine a home without books. She embodies a slightly old-fashioned mindset, believing that good books should serve as reference material and be loaned out to be read again and again. Books hold great personal significance for Jette, and many of them have been passed down to her.

The soul of the home is reflected in the diverse collections of art, books, glassware, porcelain, baskets, silver frames, and wooden figures. I am captivated by the abundance of everything. There are stacks of throws, a sea of cushions, porcelain arranged in neat piles, a well-filled bookshelf that has a delightful sense of organised chaos, a profusion of silver frames, artwork displayed side by side, and overwhelming bouquets of country roses—even a towering wobbly stack of pink knit sweaters that is enviable. It's clear that the inhabitants exude abundance, passion, aesthetics, and impeccable taste.

As for the many frames that Jette collects, she explains: "A hundred years ago, the frame was a significant part of the artwork. Today, the frame should draw as little attention as possible. It's a shame. The right frame can do a lot for a picture. The frame can support the art."

While we're on the subject of art and paintings, one of Jette's other favourite elements is portraits—both old and new—and she has a particular soft spot for the old Golden Age painters. The portraits above the sofa depict family members from the past. They have always been part of her life and previously hung in Jette's grandparents' home. She has always been fascinated by them and feels fortunate to be the one who inherited them.

"I love both old and new art. Art should resonate with you the first time you see it. When it comes to art, I believe one should not focus on potential value appreciation or investment; instead, it should be something that brings joy to look at every single day. That alone can be a worthwhile investment. I am very fond of works by Cathrine Raben Davidsen. She is a younger artist, yet her work has a very Renaissance feel. I can always find room for another piece by Cathrine Raben Davidsen or a small painting by Christen Købke."

Best of all is seeing how elegantly the home's authenticity and original details—primarily the windows—have been preserved, as they are among the most vulnerable aspects of old architecture. While it is essential to bring the villa up to modern standards, this is often done too aggressively. Fortunately, that is not the case here.

Jette is pleased that only three families have lived in the villa since its construction, which means there are not too many layers of paint or damaged plaster. The floors were beautifully polished, and the original ring beam structure was intact when she and her husband, Kim, purchased the house. However, despite the new owners' desire to preserve the original character of the home, they spent six months renovating and preparing the house for a family in the 2000s.

The couple merged two rooms into one large bathroom, updated the electrical system, opened up the kitchen for a seamless flow with the dining area, and installed a new custom kitchen. They also painted and restored the woodwork to perfection. Jette mixed the colours for all the walls in the house, selecting hues that contain both a hint of green and a bit of grey, which creates a pleasant feel and adds warmth to the very high walls.

Afterwards, they turned their attention to the basement and the house's second-floor large attic space with dormers and a balcony. Originally, there were only two toilets and one bathroom, which was inadequate for a family of five, prompting the addition of a new bathroom in the basement.

It sounds like quite a project, but Jette and Kim have previously renovated old houses and knew exactly what was required.

"We spent a long time finding the right craftspeople. You can tell when a craftsperson has an aesthetic sense. For example, when they don't suggest replacing old window frames with new ones but instead take pride in preserving the originals by thoroughly sanding them and applying linseed oil. Similarly, we had the old cast-iron grate repaired by a blacksmith, found antique porcelain socket covers, and had a railing crafted from the first to the second floor. We even managed to find an old, retired carpenter who could bend the wood in the perfect way."

"The skilled craftspeople we work with are our best partners in the creative process. I hold great respect for artisans who take pride in doing excellent work, those who master the traditional techniques. I am glad there are still some who can. Unfortunately, there are far too few. We must truly cherish good craftsmanship."

Jette finds inspiration for her projects in unexpected places. It could be a trip to Paris, where the flooring at Versailles leaves her in awe, or the paintings and colours in an old tea shop. She also draws ideas from stores that specialise in vintage bookbinding and museums around the world.

FRANSKE FORBINDELSER
FRANSKE FORBINDELSER
RITZ

SKE FORBINDELSER
SKE FORBINDELSER

Jette Witzke

Jette worked in the media industry for 18 years. She was a partner in various agencies and loved her job, but she always knew that one day she would pursue her greatest passion: the fine craftsmanship involved in interior design and house renovations.

In autumn 2016, she realized her dream and started the company Le Metièr, a showroom from which she manages larger construction projects for private clients. The name of her business directly translates to 'the craft' in French, reflecting her dedication to quality workmanship. Today, she combines her experience in project management with her immense interest in creating spaces and enhancing the quality of life for her clients.

When Jette provides advice, she focuses on being true to the property's era and age—as she puts it: "It's pointless to create a chateau style in a functionalist villa, or functionalism in an old palace villa." Another key focus for her is creating a cohesive thread throughout the decor. Everything must connect, from tiles in the bathroom to the kitchen and flooring, style, and colours. She thoroughly immerses herself in her clients' lives, needs, and desires to create optimal settings. When assisting families with children at home, she thinks practically, ensuring that functionality doesn't compromise aesthetics.

Jette works with a consistent team of craftspeople—professionals who share her high standards for quality and aesthetics. She often finds that clients are surprised by the quality of life that comes from living in spaces where colours and materials are harmoniously coordinated.

"Just as a word gains its clear meaning only in relation to other words, individual colours gain their clear expression and precise significance only in relation to other colours."

–

Johannes Itten (1888-1967), Swiss Painter, Designer, Teacher, and Theorist

INTERMEZZO

Books

In addition to being fantastic colour generators in the home, books possess **a unique charm**. They reveal who you are. A home without books quickly feels bare and somewhat bland, while a home filled with books reflects the interests and depth of its inhabitants. However, a bookshelf can also easily become overwhelming and draw too much attention.

I have come to realise that not all my books can stay in the living room, leading me to choose a smaller shelf that displays only monochromatic books in that space, while the colourful ones have been banished to a larger bookshelf in my office. It's not a situation I'm particularly proud of—I simply found it too distracting for my taste.

When it comes to **bookshelves**, remember that it's not only about what you place on the shelves and how you arrange the books; the shelf or cabinet itself also plays a crucial role. A built-in carpenter's bookshelf that stretches from floor to ceiling, possibly designed around double doors and painted in a lovely colour, can be exquisite. Wooden shelves, whether new or vintage, are also irresistible, just as an antique French display cabinet with glass doors can beautifully frame your books. Steer clear of disappointing white laminate bookcases; it's often better to create a tall stack of books on the floor instead. (See Funky Reflections, p.114)

You have the option to **arrange your books** by colour on the shelf, though this is a bit too staged for my liking. In contrast, organising them by height provides a lovely sense of order. I categorise my non-fiction books by subject, placing the tallest ones on the far left and continuing from there. If you have smaller decorative items that you'd also like to incorporate, you can push some books back and place a small object in the resulting space. At the end of a stack of books, you can set a vase, sculpture, or another decorative piece that adds life to the arrangement. Dedicating an entire section of your bookshelf to a unique piece of pottery or a fine sculpture can also be **visually impactful**. (See Country Ambience, p.164)

If you decide to have a **custom bookshelf** built, make sure to evaluate your book collection before determining the height of the shelves. It's nice to have space for taller books to stand upright. If not, it's perfectly acceptable for the tallest books to be stacked horizontally. It's also fine to place a couple of books flat on top of those that are arranged vertically.

A good tip is to place the tallest and thickest books at the bottom of the shelf, while the smallest and thinnest books should be positioned higher up. And remember, your bookshelf's beauty is determined by the **items you display in it**. If you need space for photo albums and folders with paperwork, avoid unattractive coloured plastic binders, opting instead for solid-coloured fabric-bound folders or boxes.

Books can also be integrated into your decor in various ways beyond just being housed on shelves. They can be stacked and placed in **windowsills or on coffee tables**. This is an effective strategy to achieve a personalised and cosy atmosphere, but it works best with books of substantial weight, thickness, and size. Stack three to four beautiful design or architecture books on top of each other, starting with the largest book on the bottom, and consider finishing the arrangement with a small ceramic bowl or a candlestick with a candle on top. (See African Vibes, p.220 and Pastel Elegance, p.254)

Acknowledgements

I would like to thank my editor, Carolijn Domensino, for encouraging me to write this book, and for her invaluable guidance throughout the process. You captured my imagination during a magical moment as I roamed through the architecture and colours of La Recoleta in Buenos Aires, Argentina—one of the world's most famous cemeteries, where Evita Perón is buried. Shortly after our conversation, I began to compose this book in my mind.

A heartfelt thank you also goes to Mikkel Adsbøl, Kira Brandt, Frederik Johs, Mathilde Schmidt, and Rigetta Klint for your beautiful and vibrant photography, and, of course, to all the homeowners who allowed us a glimpse into their colourful universes.

Credits

Concept – text – styling: Katrine Martensen-Larsen
Editing: Heather Sills
Book design: Tina De Souter Bookdesign

Photography:
Frederik Johs: *Futuristic Narnia, Scandic Oriental*
Kira Brandt: Coastal Calmness, Funky Reflections, African Vibes, Pastel Elegance, mood board images p.9, p.13-28
Mathilde Schmidt: *p.4*
Mikkel Adsbøl: *Colour Extravaganza, Island Delight, Country Ambience, mood board images p.87, p.111, p.137, p.189, cover and back cover image*
Rigetta Klint /Håndværk bookazine: *p.10, p.11*

D/2025/45/375 – NUR 454
ISBN: 978 90 209 7345 7
www.lannoo.com

If you have any questions or comments about the material in this book, please do not hesitate to contact our editorial team: art@lannoo.com.